Religions of the World

Series Editor: Ninian Smart

CHINESE
RELIGIOUS TRADITIONS

Joseph A. Adler

Kenyon College, Gambier, Ohio

Prentice
Hall

Prentice Hall Inc., Upper Saddle River, NJ 07458

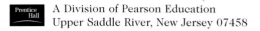 A Division of Pearson Education
Upper Saddle River, New Jersey 07458

10 9 8 7 6 5 4 3 2 1

ISBN 0-13-091163-1

 This book was designed and produced by
LAURENCE KING PUBLISHING LTD, London
www.laurenceking.co.uk

Editorial work by Christine Davis, Richard Mason, Matthew Taylor
Design by Karen Stafford
Map by Andrea Fairbrass
Calligraphy by Shui Yim Tse, with thanks to the Society for the Study of
Chinese Religions
Picture research by Julia Ruxton
Printed in Hong Kong

Reviewers Whalen Lai, University of California, Davis; Vivian-Lee Nyitray,
University of California, Riverside; Angela Zito, New York University; Eric
Reinders, Emory University

Picture Credits

Cover Sally and Richard Greenhill, London; *page 44* Art Archive,
London/British Museum, London; *page 70* Thames & Hudson
Ltd./private collection; photo: Jeff Teasdale; *page 82* Cultural Relics
Publishing House, Beijing; *page 87* Graham Harrison, Thame, Oxon;
page 95 National Palace Museum, Taiwan; *page 106* Tour Bookstore,
Beijing; *page 114* Joseph Adler

Contents

5: Early Modern China: Song through Early Qing 90

6: Modern China 110

Foreword

Religions of the World

The informed citizen or student needs a good overall knowledge of our small but complicated world. Fifty years ago you might have neglected religions. Now, however, we are shrewder and can see that religions and ideologies not only form civilizations but directly influence international events. These brief books provide succinct, balanced, and informative guides to the major faiths and one volume also introduces the changing religious scene as we enter the new millennium.

Today we want not only to be informed, but to be stimulated by the life and beliefs of the diverse and often complex religions of today's world. These insightful and accessible introductions allow you to explore the riches of each tradition—to understand its history, its beliefs and practices, and also to grasp its influence upon the modern world. The books have been written by a team of excellent and, on the whole, younger scholars who represent a new generation of writers in the field of religious studies. While aware of the political and historical influences of religion these authors aim to present the religion's spiritual side in a fresh and interesting way. So whether you are interested simply in descriptive knowledge of a faith, or in exploring its spiritual message, you will find these introductions invaluable.

The emphasis in these books is on the modern period, because every religious tradition has transformed itself in the face of the traumatic experiences of the last two hundred years or more. Colonialism, industrialization, nationalism, revivals of religion, new religions, world wars, revolutions, and social transformations have not left faith unaffected and have drawn on religious and anti-religious forces to reshape our world. Modern technology in the last 25 years—from the Boeing 747 to the world wide web—has made our globe seem a much smaller place. Even the moon's magic has been captured by technology.

We meet in these books people of the modern period as a sample of the many changes over the last few centuries. At the same time, each book provides a valuable insight into the different dimensions of the religion: its teachings, narratives, organizations, rituals, and experiences. In touching on these features, each volume gives a rounded view of the tradition, enabling you to understand what it means to belong to a particular faith. As the native American proverb has it: "Never judge a person without walking a mile in his moccasins."

To assist you further in your exploration, a number of useful reference aids are included. Each book contains a chronology, map, glossary, pronunciation guide, list of festivals, annotated reading list, and index; while a selection of images provide examples of religious art, symbols, and contemporary practices.

I hope you will find these introductions enjoyable and illuminating. Brevity is supposed to be the soul of wit: it can also turn out to be what we need in the first instance in introducing cultural and spiritual themes.

Ninian Smart
Santa Barbara, 1998

Preface

China has been the major cultural center of East Asia for about 2000 years, and our knowledge of its religious traditions extends back at least another 1500 years before that. Over that span of 3500 years, China has produced two major systems of religious thought and practice (Confucianism and Daoism) and has thoroughly transformed a third (Buddhism), while its popular, unsystematized religious practices have simultaneously developed as a fourth, semi-independent tradition. All four of these religious traditions have not only shaped Chinese culture but have also influenced the neighboring cultures of Korea, Japan, and parts of Southeast Asia. Today they are becoming much better-known in the West, through scholarship and through the presence of Chinese communities outside of Asia.

In our increasingly interconnected world, in which political and geographic boundaries are becoming less and less significant and scholarship is continually advancing, new perspectives in cross-cultural studies are constantly being generated. The late Ninian Smart, under whom I was very fortunate to study at the University of California at Santa Barbara, was keenly aware that religions are products of particular cultures, and that the continuing life of those cultures prevents us from closing the books on their religious traditions. Hence the need periodically to reexamine the religions of the world.

Tracing the development of four religious traditions over 3500 years in a book as short as this has not been an easy task. I am grateful to the staff at Laurence King Publishing in London, especially Richard Mason and Christine Davis, for helping me to meet the requirements of this series. I would also like to acknowledge the stimulation and insights I have gained from my students at Kenyon College, where I have taught the course on which this book is based for fifteen years. That course was powerfully influenced by my graduate studies with Robert Gimello and Tu Weiming, who may recognize some of their insights in these pages. Finally, I owe a great deal to Ninian Smart, whose clarity of thinking, sensitivity of interpretation, and boundless goodwill and good cheer were models I will always treasure. This book is dedicated to him.

Joseph A. Adler
November 2001

Traditional/Mythic History of China

The figures in the first two groups below are mythic "culture-heroes" or historicized gods to whom many of the characteristic features of Chinese culture are attributed. The Three Dynasties are also mythic in the sense that they were later seen as symbolic of fundamental cultural values. The Shang and Zhou dynasties are both mythic and historic.

The Three Sovereigns (*San huang*)

- Fuxi ("Subduer of Animals"), 29th century B.C.E.: invented hunting and fishing implements, animal sacrifice, and *Yijing* hexagram divination.
- Shennong ("Divine Farmer"), 28th century B.C.E.: invented agriculture.
- Huangdi ("Yellow Emperor"), 27th century B.C.E.: writing, silk, boats, and carts invented under his rule.

The Three Sages (*San sheng*)

- Yao, 24th century B.C.E.: central government, calendar, rites, and music attributed to him; he passed over his own son to select Shun as his successor, based on merit.
- Shun, 23rd century B.C.E.: known for his filial devotion despite having cruel parents; also passed over his son to select Yu as his successor on basis of merit.
- Yu, 22nd century B.C.E.: controlled the flooding of the Yellow River; selected his son Qi as successor because people were attracted to him, thus founding the first dynasty (Xia).

The Three Dynasties (*San dai*)

- Xia, 22nd–18th century B.C.E.
    Virtuous founder: Yu.
    Evil last king: Jie (according to later doctrine of the Mandate of Heaven).

·················· **DOCUMENTATION BEGINS** ··················

- Shang (Yin): 18th–12th century B.C.E. (traditional dates), or 14th–11th century B.C.E. (modern estimate).
    Last capital at Yin (Anyang), hence alternative name.
    Virtuous founder: Tang.
    Evil last king: Zhou.

- Zhou: 1122 (traditional) or 1045 (modern)–221 B.C.E.
    Western Zhou: capital at Changian (modern Xian).
        King Wen: imprisoned under King Zhou of Shang; wrote hexagram texts of *Yijing*.
        King Wu: son of King Wen; overthrew Shang.
        Duke of Zhou: King Wu's brother; regent for King Wu's son King Cheng.
    Eastern Zhou: capital at Luoyang.
        722–479 B.C.E.: "Spring and Autumn" period (Confucius 551–479 B.C.E.).
        479–221 B.C.E.: "Warring States" period.

Major Documented Periods in Chinese History

Dynasty or period	Dates	Major developments in religion
Shang (Yin)	14th–11th century B.C.E.	Ritual: divination and sacrifice by Shang kings.
Western Zhou	1045–771 B.C.E.	Doctrine of Mandate of Heaven; beginnings of Five Classics.
Eastern Zhou "Spring and Autumn" period "Warring States" period	771–221 B.C.E. 722–479 B.C.E. 479–221 B.C.E.	Confucius (Classical Confucianism). Mencius, Xunzi (Classical Confucianism). "Laozi," Zhuangzi (Classical Daoism).
Qin	221–207 B.C.E.	Legalism as government ideology.
Former Han	206 B.C.E.–9 C.E.	Confucianism becomes state orthodoxy.
Latter Han	23–220 C.E.	Beginnings of Daoist religion; Buddhism enters China.
Six Dynasties (disunity)	220–589	Daoism and Buddhism flourish; Confucianism declines.
Sui	589–618	New schools of Buddhism: Pure Land, Tiantai, Huayan, and Chan.
Tang	618–906	845: suppression of Buddhism. Precursors of Neo-Confucian revival (for example Han Yu).
Five Dynasties (disunity)	907–960	Daoism continues to develop.
Song Northern: 960–1127 Southern: 1127–1279	960–1279 1127 1279	Confucian revival (Neo-Confucianism); Pure Land and Chan Buddhism flourish. Jurchen take over northern China. Mongols take over all of China.
Yüan (Mongol)	1279–1368	Zhu Xi's Neo-Confucianism becomes orthodox.
Ming	1368–1644	Wang Yang-ming's Neo-Confucianism.
Qing (Manchu)	1644–1911	Critical study (*kaozheng*) of ancient texts; Western learning enters China; Tibetan Buddhism supported by Manchu rulers.
Republic of China	1911–	Confucian bureaucratic and education systems dropped; traditional religions maintained. 1949: defeated by Communist revolution, driven to Taiwan, martial law until 1987.
People's Republic of China (Republic of China now in Taiwan)	1949–	Under Mao Zedong (d. 1976), Confucianism discredited; temples destroyed; atheism established as official doctrine. 1966–76: "Great Proletarian Cultural Revolution." Under Deng Xiaoping (d. 1997) and Jiang Zemin: Confucianism regains some legitimacy; Daoism and Buddhism partially restored; beginnings of revival of popular religion.

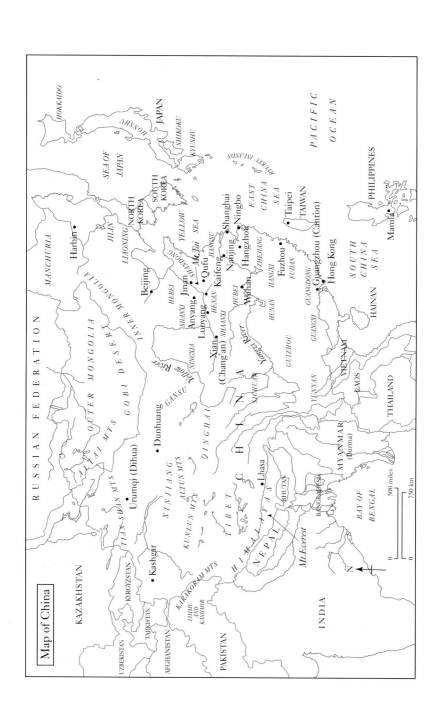

Map of China

The young woman just inside the large main gate of Longshan Temple shuffles the bamboo divination slips (about two feet long and half an inch wide) standing in the brass canister and chooses one. She walks quickly to the midline of the temple, just inside the large main entrance gate, and faces the statue of **Guanyin**, the **Bodhisattva** of Compassion, who occupies the place of honor in a separate structure toward the rear of the open courtyard. The woman places her hands together in front of her face, holding the divination slip vertically between them, and prays for about half a minute to Guanyin. She then drops onto the stone floor her moon blocks— two red-painted wooden crescents, about three inches long, convex on one side and flat on the other. Picking them up, she notes whether they fell flat sides up, convex sides up, or one of each. She walks back to the canister, replaces the divination slip, shuffles them again, and chooses another one. After returning to her spot in the center she prays and throws her moon blocks again. She does this half a dozen times before the way the moon blocks fall indicates that the slip she has chosen is the right one for her today (one up and one down is a positive response, and two or three positive responses in a row are usually considered necessary).

She notes the number written on the divination slip, puts it back in the canister, and walks over to the corner, just inside the left front entrance of the temple. There stands a cabinet with 108 small drawers, like those containing the herbs and other medicines in a traditional Chinese drugstore. She opens drawer number 98 and pulls out a slip of paper on which are various pieces of advice concerning family matters, business, and so forth. After reading the divination response she walks briskly through the courtyard to one of the rear exits.

Meanwhile, the hundred or so other people in the temple that day are worshipping in their own ways. Some, like her, are using divination slips in combination with moon blocks. Others have brought offerings of fruit, cooking oil, crackers, or packaged sweets to offer to any or all of the various deities enshrined in Longshan. After putting their offerings on one of several large tables in the courtyard, most of them pray while holding burning incense sticks instead of divination slips. Then they insert the incense sticks into the sand inside one of the huge open pots, which emit thick white clouds of pungent smoke. Some just burn incense and pray. Many of them throw their moon blocks to see whether their offerings and/or prayers have been received favorably by the deities. Some—mostly older women—are kneeling on padded stools in front of the offering tables, or directly in front of the altars of the deities, and reading or chanting Buddhist **sutras**. Since the chief deity at Longshan is Guanyin, most of them are reading the *Guanyin Sutra*, which is actually a chapter from the longer **Lotus Sutra**.

Longshan ("Dragon Mountain") Temple is one of the oldest and most popular temples in Taibei, Taiwan. But the activities seen here every day of the week are also seen in thousands of other temples in Chinese communities throughout the world. Longshan was originally, and still is, primarily a Buddhist temple. The front gate leading into the outer courtyard has Buddhist swastikas among its opulent decorations,[1] and the chief deity is Guanyin, a bodhisattva. Bodhisattvas in the Buddhist tradition are enlightened, compassionate beings dedicated to helping others achieve enlightenment and an end to suffering. Guanyin is the Chinese equivalent of Avalokitesvara, the original Sanskrit name of this bodhisattva. She is the most popular deity in East Asia, especially among women.

The deity whose altar and image are directly behind Guanyin's—in the position of second-highest honor—is **Mazu**, the most popular deity in Taiwan. She is equally popular along the southeast coast of China, where she lived as the daughter of a fisherman during the late tenth century. She died young, unmarried, and later became a goddess. Over the course of several centuries her fame and power grew so much that she was given official titles by the imperial government, culminating in her present exalted title, **Tianshang Shengmu**, or "Holy Mother in Heaven."

Mazu is not a Buddhist deity; she is part of what scholars call "popular" or "folk" religion (**minjian zongjiao**). But this is strictly an academic classification, not a term generally used by the people who practice it. They themselves refer to their *activities* simply as "worshipping the gods" (*bai shen*), or just "worshipping" (*bai-bai*). The gods they worship may have Buddhist, Daoist, or Confucian affiliations, or none of these. In fact, Chinese popular religion has no proper name—it is not an -ism. It is better to think of Chinese popular religion as a common underlying set of beliefs and practices—like the divination at Longshan—that gives rise (along with external influences such as Buddhism, which came from India) to the more specific strands of canonical Chinese religion: Confucianism, Daoism, and Buddhism. These "Three Teachings" (*sanjiao*)—which perhaps we could call the "three -isms"—have, in turn, had a reciprocal influence on popular religion.

Guanyin and Mazu are not the only deities enshrined at Longshan. There is **Guandi**, who lived in the third century C.E. and is now the god of war and business. Guandi is loosely associated with Confucianism, as he is famous for his loyalty to the Han royal house after it had lost control of its empire—and loyalty (*zhong*) is one of the important Confucian virtues. And there is **Wenchang**, the god of literature and success in examinations, who is associated with both Confucianism and Daoism. Wenchang is especially popular among students preparing to take the college entrance examinations in June. On the same June day that the young woman was praying to Guanyin, Wenchang's offering table was overflowing with food offerings.

Typically, people come to Longshan to worship not just one of these gods but all of them. Each god has his or her specialty, but most people recognize different aspects of their lives in which they would appreciate divine assistance. There is very little jealousy among the gods and goddesses of Chinese culture, and likewise very little notion that religious belief and practice must focus on a single tradition. Some people consider themselves Buddhists, and there are Daoist and Buddhist monks, nuns, and priests, but most people simply worship the gods, ghosts, and ancestors without identifying themselves as "members" of a specific religion. To the extent that religion is one of the factors that people use to construct their identities—and that is certainly one of its important functions—it signifies "membership" in Chinese culture.

The religious landscape of China is often described in terms of three religions—Confucianism, Daoism, and Buddhism—each of which has canons of sacred texts or *jing* (classic, scripture, or *sutra*), ritual practices, and recognized lineages of sages or teachers. While there is some overlap among them, and in general they do not demand exclusive membership and rejection of the teachings of the others, they are relatively easy to distinguish conceptually as discrete traditions. Popular religion is harder to define, because it freely borrows from all of the three teachings while for the most part lacking their textual elements. Nevertheless it is a widely used category among scholars of Chinese religion, and scholarship in popular religion is rapidly growing.

In this book the three teachings and popular religion will therefore comprise the four central "traditions" to be examined, in a chronological framework. As much as possible we will look at each of the four traditions in each historical period, although the flourishing and decline of each tradition (as well as certain gaps in the historical record) will allow us to emphasize them in different chapters. But it is important to bear in mind that only rarely in Chinese history have the lines between the four traditions been sharply drawn.

Confucianism

The man we call "Confucius" lived in the sixth and fifth centuries B.C.E. and is generally called Kongzi, or "Master Kong," in Chinese. He seems to have been an itinerant teacher with a small but devoted band of followers, called *ru*, a word that came to mean something like "scholar." The *ru* were known in ancient China as experts on the written cultural tradition (*wen*), and in particular on the elaborate codes of "ritual" (*li*) that governed the official and private conduct of the ruling aristocracy. But Confucius' teachings contained the beginnings of a system of thought and behavior that developed into a sophisticated ethico-religious tradition. In this system, human beings are understood as essentially social beings, and human fulfillment involves perfecting the moral nature of both the individual and the society. Confucius thought that the ideal socio-ethical-political order, the *Dao* or Way, had been realized in the past but was now lost, and his "mission" was to revive it.

After Confucius' death in 479 B.C.E. his teachings were propagated by his followers and entered the currents of intellectual debates. In the second century B.C.E. Confucianism was adopted by the Han dynasty (206 B.C.E.–220 C.E.) as the intellectual basis for its system of government and its educational program for training officials. Education in China came to be conceived largely in Confucian terms, enabling the influence of Confucianism to spread throughout all levels of Chinese society—even among the illiterate masses. In Taiwan today, Confucius' birthday (September 28) is celebrated as Teachers' Day, a national holiday.

After the fall of the Han dynasty, Confucianism lost much of its philosophical vitality for several centuries, although it remained the state orthodoxy and the basis of the educational system, and it was fully integrated with the system of religious rituals conducted by the emperor and lower officials. In the Song dynasty (960–1279) there was a revival and reformulation of the tradition, with some influence from Buddhism and Daoism. This movement, which came to be known in the West as "Neo-Confucianism," gave Confucianism new appeal not only as a system of thought but also as a religious way of life for most Chinese intellectuals. It remained the dominant school of Chinese philosophical thought until the twentieth century, although other currents have played important roles. Chinese intellectuals today—whether in mainland China, Taiwan, other Chinese communities in Asia, or the West—draw upon the whole range of world philosophies. Still, Confucian principles and values remain extraordinarily deeply rooted in Chinese society.

Daoism

The origins of Daoism are unclear, but it has traditionally been associated with the sage Laozi and his short, enigmatic text the *Laozi* or ***Daodejing*** ("Classic of the Way and its Power"). Laozi is said to have been an older contemporary of Confucius, but scholars since the early twentieth century have generally agreed that he is a purely mythic figure and that the *Laozi* is not the product of a single author, but was compiled from several sources during the third century B.C.E. Early Daoism evolved as something like a harmony to the dominant melody of Confucianism in Chinese culture. While Confucianism stressed that human beings are essentially social beings, the early Daoist classics— the *Daode jing* and the ***Zhuangzi*** (named for its primary author, who lived in the fourth and third centuries B.C.E.)—stressed instead that human beings are essentially *natural* beings, and that human fulfillment lay in harmonizing our thinking and behavior with the Way (*dao*), which they conceived as the patterns and rhythms of nature. There may have also been, at this time, a tradition of personal cultivation and meditation that was used to develop one's spiritual capacity to understand and harmonize with the Dao. Very little is known of this, but certain texts, some predating the compilation of the *Laozi*, seem to outline such a system.

However, in the second century C.E., a new series of revelations—from a deified Laozi—sparked the development of Daoism into a full-fledged religious community, complete with gods, a sacred textual canon, priests, rituals, and meditation. Later revelations resulted in a Daoist canon comprising some 1400 titles, several sub-traditions or sects, and considerable popularity throughout medieval and early modern Chinese history. The ultimate goal of Daoist religious practice became the achievement of immortality, with the help of a huge pantheon of gods and immortals. The focus of Daoist meditation and spiritual cultivation is the individual's psycho-physical-spiritual substance, or *qi*, the stuff of which all existing things (including gods and spirits) are composed. Through this focus on the body/mind/spirit Daoism influenced the development of traditional Chinese medicine, still widely practiced today.

Today there are two major sects of Daoism, one with a hereditary priesthood and the other with a monastic system of training monks and nuns. The primary role of Daoist priests today, outside their monasteries, is to perform specific rituals for individuals, families, and communities. They are essentially the priesthood of Chinese popular religion, although they perform that role only when hired for specific occasions.

Buddhism

The founder of Buddhism lived at roughly the same time as Confucius, but in northern India. His name was Siddhartha Gautama and he was born a prince but renounced the life of privilege to become a wandering ascetic, seeking personal liberation from the frustration and suffering of life. After several years of intense effort (according to traditional accounts) he gave up extreme asceticism for a more balanced approach to liberation, focusing on meditation. Eventually his meditation led to an enlightenment experience in which he saw the cause of suffering and its solution. After this he was called the **Buddha,** or "Awakened One." He developed his insight into a comprehensive lifestyle comprising ethical behavior, the understanding of certain truths about the causes and conditions of all existing things, and the focused effort to achieve purification of the mind and liberation from the mental habits that bind us to suffering. He also founded a religious community, known as the **Sangha**, composed of monks, nuns, laymen, and laywomen, all of whom were followers of the Way or Path that the Buddha had set out.

Buddhism entered China at roughly the turn of the first millennium, traveling primarily with merchants on the Indian branch of the Silk Road into Central Asia and then eastward into China. At first seen by the Chinese as an alien, socially irresponsible tradition, Buddhism took several hundred years of gradual assimilation to become a fully Chinese tradition. Several entirely new schools of Buddhism developed in China and later spread to Korea and Japan. By the ninth century C.E. Buddhism had become popular enough to be seen as a threat to the traditional Confucian fabric of Chinese society, and its tax-exempt monastic communities were becoming a drain on the economy. This resulted in an official suppression of Buddhism in the ninth century, followed by the revival of Confucianism in the Song dynasty. But the official suppression lasted only a few years, and Buddhism re-emerged as an influence, especially the new school known as **Chan** (Zen in Japanese). Since the Song dynasty, Buddhism has thrived in China—at least until the Communist suppression of all religions in the second half of the twentieth century—while in Taiwan and other Chinese communities it has flourished continuously. Recently Taiwan has seen a tremendous growth of lay Buddhism, with a strong focus on social welfare activity.

Popular Religion

The earliest known form of Chinese religion is that of the aristocracy of the Shang dynasty (fourteenth–eleventh centuries B.C.E.); we know virtually nothing of any religious practices of the common people of that distant era. This situation improves slowly as we move forward in history. For example, for the era known as the "classical" period, during which Confucius lived and the Daoist classics were compiled and written, what sketchy information we have is gleaned from such texts as the *Classic of Odes*, which contains folk songs that probably reflect some of the concerns of common people. But by the time of the Song dynasty, primary sources are extensive enough to enable us to construct a fairly rich portrait of ordinary life and popular religion.

Scholars today are increasingly coming to realize that the barrier between the "élite" and "popular" levels of Chinese culture was more porous than previously thought. During the Song dynasty, for example, the literati who developed the Neo-Confucian tradition practiced divination, sacrifice, and ancestor worship, which are the staples of popular religious practice. There were always avenues of mutual influence between the literate and non-literate classes in China. Both the intellectual speculation and the religious practices of the educated élite reflected the worldview of the average Chinese peasant in certain ways, while the social mores of ordinary people display the basic Confucian principles that have "trickled down" through the educational system and government bureaucracies. Of course there were significant differences between the interests and sensibilities of the average peasant and the average scholar–official, but there was an underlying commonality in their religious worldviews that allowed for fluid exchange and mutual fertilization throughout Chinese history.

The details of popular religion—which gods are worshipped, specific festivals and rituals, and beliefs about gods, ghosts, and ancestors—have varied over time and from place to place (as they still do). The discussion at the beginning of this chapter will suffice at this point as a basic characterization of popular religion, to be elaborated on in later chapters.

Themes

In the chapters that follow a number of themes will frequently surface. The first is the notion that change and transformation are fundamental to the nature of things, including human life. As we shall see, the Chinese in this sense have consistently understood reality in exactly the opposite way from the the predominant Western philosophical tradition, which has been strongly influenced by Plato's claim that what is real is that which does not change.

The harmony and continuity of the family, which has traditionally been the fundamental unit of social life, is reflected on many levels of Chinese religion, especially in Confucianism and popular religion. Ancestor worship is one of the most visible manifestations of this pattern, as departed ancestors are just as much members of the family as the living members.

There has always been a close relationship between religion and politics in China. As early as the second millennium B.C.E. the ruler was responsible for maintaining a harmonious relationship between the realm of gods and ancestors and the human realm. In later periods, governments through the beginning of the twentieth century not only continued this religious role but also tried to control religious institutions and movements as much as possible. An extreme level of control has continued into the twenty-first century in mainland China, but in Taiwan and other Chinese communities today there is little political control of religion.

Finally, perhaps the most overarching theme in the history of Chinese religion is the "unity of Heaven and humanity" (*tian ren heyi*), or the non-duality of the transcendent and the mundane. We see this in the linkage maintained by rulers between the divine and human realms, in Confucian and Daoist philosophical ideas about the Dao, in Chinese Buddhist concepts of enlightenment, and in popular religious worship of gods, ghosts, and ancestors. As a general pattern of thought and behavior, we will see how this **non-dualism** of transcendence and immanence can be conceived as a fundamental ordering principle underlying all the varieties of Chinese worldviews that we will be exploring.

The Shang and Western Zhou Periods

Shang Religion

There are archaeological traces of religious practice in China dating to the Neolithic period (c. 12,000–2000 B.C.E.), but the earliest documented form of Chinese religion is from the bronze age, during the period known in Chinese history as the Shang dynasty (c. 1300–1045 B.C.E.). The evidence for this was discovered in the  early twentieth century, after inscribed "dragon bones" being sold as medicine in traditional Chinese pharmacies were found to have originated in the area of Anyang, in Henan province (east central China), where farmers had dug them out of their fields. Archaeological excavations begun in 1928 led to the discovery of the last capital of the Shang dynasty, a city called Yin. The bones turned out to be the material used by the Shang kings to perform divination to their gods and ancestors. They are therefore called "oracle bones," and their written inscriptions, which are an early form of the Chinese characters still used today, constitute the earliest historical documents in Chinese history.

The Shang dynasty controlled an area in northeast China north and south of the Yellow River and roughly between the modern cities of Luoyang and Jinan. Smaller "statelets" occupied territories within this area, controlled by local chieftains who acknowledged the power and authority of the Shang. The remains of some of the Shang city walls suggest that they had the power to mobilize large workforces over sustained periods of time. They had an extremely well-developed and sophisticated bronzecasting industry, which produced an astonishing assortment of complex and beautiful ritual vessels for offerings of wine and food to the royal ancestors. Members of the royal families were buried in elaborate tombs stocked with articles for use in the afterlife; some kings were buried with horses and servants, who were apparently sacrificed for the occasion. The religion of the Shang aristocracy centered on the king and his relationship with his departed ancestors. In a heavenly realm that paralleled the earthly royal court, these ancestors served under a god called **Di** (Lord) or **Shang Di** (High Lord or Lord Above).[1] There were also lesser gods, who personified the powers of mountains, rivers, and other natural features. Di had the power to control or influence natural and human phenomena, such as the weather, the success of crops, the success of royal hunting expeditions and military campaigns, and the health of the king. The king's ancestors also had power over his health, and they could also intercede on his behalf with Di himself (he was most likely conceived as being male), a position that made them extremely important in Shang theology and government.

The Shang kings had essentially a two-way channel of communication with their ancestors and Di. Through an elaborate system of sacrificial offerings, mainly to their ancestors, they attempted to maintain good relations with their counterparts above, and through the practice of divination, using oracle bones, they determined whether their sacrifices had been well received and whether their plans would be likely to succeed. The Shang kings were thus a crucial pivot between Heaven and Earth. The welfare of the state and its people depended on the kings maintaining harmonious relations with Di and the ancestors. Affairs of state were therefore necessarily religious, and the religious practices of sacrifice and divination had inherently political implications.

The most frequent topics of divination questions included the following: (i) sacrifices (whether they had been performed properly and received with favor); (ii) military campaigns (whether Di would aid the king, whether alliances should be made); (iii) hunting expeditions (where to hunt, whether the hunt would be successful); (iv) excursions (whether any misfortune would befall the king); (v) the coming day, night, or ten-day week (whether any misfortune would occur); (vi) the weather; (vii) agriculture (when to plant or harvest, reasons for crop failures); (viii) sickness (which ancestor was cursing the king, what sacrifice would be required for a cure); (ix) childbirth (whether the birth would be successful, whether the child would be a son); (x) dreams (their significance and which ancestors had sent

An inscribed Shang-dynasty oracle bone, in this case a bovine scapula or shoulder blade. These large bones were used for their relatively flat surfaces on which divination inscriptions could be written.

them); (xi) settlement building (whether Di approved of a particular site).[2]

The method of divination used by the Shang kings involved the burning and cracking of bones. These could be of two kinds: the scapula (shoulder blade) of cattle or the plastron (bottom bone) of tortoises, about one foot in length. Both provided relatively broad, flat areas on which inscriptions could be made.

First, the bone was dried and a series of hollows gouged or bored into it in one or more double columns. Then the king or a divination specialist would announce the question or "charge" being put to the oracle; for example, "We will receive the millet harvest." Then he would place a red-hot stick or poker into the hollow until the bone cracked, the crack appearing on the opposite side of the bone. The shaping of the hollows resulted in cracks in the shape of a sideways letter T (⊣ or ⊦). The written word for this divination procedure has roughly the same shape; in modern Mandarin Chinese it is pronounced *bu*, but in Shang times it may have pronounced something like *puk* or *pak*, imitating the sound of the bone cracking. In many cases the diviner would then repeat the charge as a negative statement ("We will not receive the millet harvest") and would heat and crack the hollow in the parallel column. This procedure was usually repeated five or ten times.

It is not known how the cracks were interpreted. Their shape, the speed with which they appeared, or even the sounds may have been factors. The initial interpretation or reading—whether or not each crack was "auspicious" (*ji*)—was made by the diviner (or the king) who had performed the cracking and, if auspicious, would be inscribed on the bone along with the number of the crack. This would be the basis for a more specific prognostication by the king regarding what should be done or what would happen; for example, "The king said, 'We will receive the harvest,'" or "The king said, 'It will rain.'"

After the prognostication was made, a record of the procedure was inscribed into the bone, including the date, the name of the diviner, the charge, in some cases the prognostication, and in fewer cases the eventual outcome of the event in question (such as "On the fifth day it rained."). Finally, the bones were polished and colored, to make the writing stand out more clearly.

These inscriptions are the source of most of our knowledge of the Shang dynasty. Over 100,000 inscribed bone fragments from the late Shang period have been discovered, most of them in pits, where they were presumably stored as official records of the activities of the Shang court. These tell us nothing about the religious beliefs or practices of common people, but some oracle bones, used but not inscribed, have been found outside the capital, suggesting that this method of divination may not have been exclusive to the royal family. And we can perhaps learn something about religion beyond the royal court from other archaeological sources, such as pottery designs and burial customs, but this would be much more speculative than what we can conclude about the religious beliefs and practices of the Shang aristocracy.

What is certain is that Shang religion displays some general themes and patterns that recur throughout the history of religion in China. Sacrifice and divination formed the central linkage between the heavenly realm and the earthly in this highly ritualistic tradition. **Sacrifice** was the ritual means of acknowledging the higher status of the gods and ancestors and providing for their needs. **Divination** was a means of receiving confirmation from the gods and ancestors that their needs were being met and of obtaining information concerning their willingness to act in favor of the royal family and the people it represented. Both practices, in one form or another, have continued to be central to Chinese popular religion up to the present day, and sacrificial offerings have also been central to Confucian and Daoist ritual.

Shang religion was very much a family affair, involving the earliest known form of Chinese ancestor worship. The ancestors were crucial intermediaries between the king and Shangdi, making possible the king's role as mediator between heaven and earth. Each day of the week was associated with a particular royal ancestor, giving time itself a sacred character.

The political dimension of Shang religion is unmistakable, and is related to the notable emphasis on the social identity of the king rather than on his individual fate or salvation. Shang aristocratic religion was not about what the individual—even the king—did in his solitude, and the king's relationship with his ancestors and with Di was important not for his personal salvation, but for the well-being of the whole state. This made religion inherently political, and politics inherently religious. The welfare of the larger social entities of family, community, and state have continued to be major concerns of Chinese religions. Conversely, Chinese governments have often been intent on controlling religion.

Shang religion had a decidedly bureaucratic dimension, reflected in the fixed schedule of sacrifices to ancestors (similar to the feast days of Roman Catholic saints), in the stipulated rules and procedures for the sacrifices, in the defined jurisdictions of the various gods and ancestors, in their hierarchical relations, and in the impersonal nature of their authority, which derived from their generational position in the family-based hierarchy of power. Many of the ancestors, for example, were simply referred to by the number of their generation (for example, "Fourth Ancestor Ding"), in sharp contrast to the strongly personal depiction of Catholic saints. The bureaucratic attitude visible in Shang religion has remained a part of Chinese religion; for example, certain popular religious deities, such as the local earth god (**tudi gong**) and the city god (**cheng huang**), are conceived as temporary holders of defined spiritual offices and can be replaced.

Finally, Shang religion was concerned with maintaining a harmony between the transcendent or sacred world (the realm of the gods and ancestors) and the mundane or profane world (the social and political realms). This was, in fact, the explicit aim of all Shang ritual. However, this harmony was not an end in itself, for it served the larger purpose of promoting the well-being of society. The king's role was the crucial pivot linking Heaven (*tian*) and Earth (*di*); the Shang king contributed to the harmony of the cosmic order.

The remarkable continuity of these themes in the history of Chinese religion should not overshadow the transformations and innovations unique to each period. Our understanding of these religious traditions must reflect the dynamic and infinitely varied phenomena of religious life. In fact, one vital lesson we can learn from Chinese religions is that real meaning and value lie in the particulars of everyday life as lived by ordinary people.

Early Zhou Religion

The Zhou people originally occupied a territory to the west of the Shang, along the Wei River, a major tributary of the Yellow River. They traced their dynasty to King Wen ("the cultured king"), whose son, King Wu ("the military king"), overthrew the Shang in the middle of the eleventh century B.C.E. King Wu died young, and since his son was too young to rule, Wu's brother the Duke of Zhou acted as regent until the young king came of age. Wen, Wu, and the Duke of Zhou were later regarded as the highest models of humane rulership, especially by Confucius and his followers. The Duke in particular was venerated, since his fiefdom was the state of Lu (just inland from the Shandong peninsula in eastern China), in which Confucius was born.

Initially Zhou culture was not as highly developed as the Shang—they had no writing, for example—but they quickly adopted Shang culture. They did not eradicate the Shang ruling family, but instead gave them a "fief," the state of Song, so that they could continue to worship and offer sacrifices to their ancestors—in exchange for loyalty to the new ruling house. Their system of government has been loosely called "feudal," but it differed from European feudalism in that Zhou peasants were not legally bound to the land, and the local lords (*gong*, or "dukes") owed allegiance to the central king (*wang*) not through law but through bonds of kinship. The king directly ruled only a small territory around the capital city, Chang'an, in the Wei River valley near present-day Xian. The Zhou kings were the first to call themselves "Son of Heaven," a term that continued to be applied to the later emperors of China until the beginning of the twentieth century, and they alone had the right (and responsibility) to make annual sacrifices to Heaven. This too was a practice that lasted until the twentieth century.

The Zhou dynasty lasted, nominally, almost 800 years—until 221 B.C.E.—but their power and their territory remained intact only until 771 B.C.E., when the king was assassinated and the capital was moved eastward to the more easily defended Luoyang. The periods corresponding to these two capitals are called Western Zhou (1045–771) and Eastern Zhou (771–221). The Western Zhou period, especially the periods of the earliest kings, was regarded by later Chinese thinkers as a golden age of enlightened, benevolent rule by sage-kings, while the Eastern Zhou was a period of increasing fragmentation, culminating in the period known as the Warring States (479–221 B.C.E.), when the last seven major states (formerly Zhou fiefdoms) battled it out until only one—the Qin—was left standing. But it was the Eastern Zhou that witnessed the origins of classical Chinese civilization. It was during this era—sometimes called the Period of the Hundred Philosophers—that Confucianism, Daoism, and many other schools of thought were born.

There are more available sources about early Zhou religion than about the Shang. In particular, it is possible to distinguish the religion of the ordinary people in the Zhou from the rituals and beliefs of the ruling élite.[3] Both groups believed in gods, ghosts, ancestors, and omens (the significance to human beings of unusual phenomena in nature) and both practiced divination, sacrifice, and exorcism. The differences between the two groups' beliefs were mostly differences in emphasis and interpretation. These distinctions begin to emerge in the Western Zhou and become clearer in the Eastern Zhou or Classical period.

The Élite

The early Zhou élite, as might be expected, were more concerned with the powerful ruling gods and political matters, while the ordinary people had more interaction with lower gods, demons, and ghosts that inhabited the world and generally made trouble for people. Along with Shang Di, the high god worshipped by the Shang kings, the Zhou also worshipped a deity called "Heaven" (**Tian**). It is likely that they worshipped Tian before their takeover of the Shang, but there is no direct evidence of this. Eventually Tian became the most widely used term for the highest spiritual being by the emerging class of intellectual élite during the Classical period. During the early Zhou it was often used synonymously with Shang Di, but it had slightly different connotations and these gradually came to predominate. Shang

Di clearly denotes a "personal" deity, one with a personal will, while Tian is a much more ambiguous term. In the early Zhou it too was probably a personal deity, but it also had impersonal connotations as the abode of the gods and ancestors. Just as in English the word "Heaven" can be used in a personal sense to refer metonymically to God ("Heaven help us"), in an impersonal sense to mean the realm of God ("Heaven is above all yet; there sits a judge that no king can corrupt"), or in a purely naturalistic sense to denote the sky or atmosphere ("The heavens opened up in a downpour"), so Tian came gradually to cover a similar range of meanings. During the Western Zhou the first two senses of Tian predominated; the third, purely naturalistic meaning was only used later by a small minority of classical philosophers.

But while the meaning of Tian (in the personal sense) overlapped that of Shang Di, Tian differed markedly in having moral connotations. As we saw, there is no hint in the Shang oracle bones of any concern with the moral character of the king or of any moral considerations on the part of Shang Di. But the ruling élite during the Western Zhou conceived of Heaven as a moral deity who had decreed that the Zhou conquer the Shang because the later Shang kings were degenerate and corrupt, whereas the Zhou kings were paragons of virtue and benevolent rulership. This belief came to be known as the Mandate of Heaven (*tianming*), and in the early classical texts it is attributed to the Duke of Zhou, brother of King Wu. The fully developed doctrine states that the authority and power to rule are given to a particular family by Heaven based on the family's virtue (*de*), and when that virtue declines, the authority to rule is taken away. This concept became, during the Classical period, the basis for the Confucian theory of dynastic change, explaining why and how the authority to rule can legitimately pass from one family line to another.

Today we might call the doctrine of the Mandate of Heaven a means of legitimizing the military overthrow of the Shang by the Zhou. Religious legitimation of political and military action is, of course, an age-old phenomenon. In ancient China it was probably the initial impetus for the growing significance of moral concerns in religious belief and practice. The doctrine of the Mandate of Heaven—and the idea that Heaven has a moral will—eventually became one of the fundamental principles of the Confucian tradition: the principle that moral values, at least in potential form, are inherent in the natural world.

Commoners

Ordinary people had less reason to be pleased with the prevailing conditions of life and therefore less reason to believe that Heaven's will was for the best. The *Classic of Odes*, for example, contains the following verse, which probably reflects the feelings of ordinary people:

> Great Heaven, unjust,
> Is sending down these exhausting disorders.
> Great Heaven, unkind,
> Is sending down these great miseries.[4]

Such sentiments, although undoubtedly not limited to the common people, are at odds with the concept of a moral, just Heaven. In general, the beliefs of Western Zhou commoners were closely tied to the agricultural cycle and to the forces that influenced it. Commoners were therefore more concerned than their élite brethren with the negative or dangerous spiritual forces inhabiting the world. In contrast to the more abstract Heaven, these forces took the form of an astonishing variety of gods, ghosts or demons, and spirits. A few of the more troublesome of these were a sacred serpent, a thorn demon, hungry ghosts, and a water-bug god. Others were more neutral or benign, such as the gods of particular mountains, rivers, and seas (usually depicted in hybrid animal or animal–human forms), earth gods (*tu shen*) of other specific localities, and the highest gods, variously called Shang Di (High Lord, the same term used during the Shang dynasty), Shang Huang (High Sovereign), and Shang Shen (High God).[5]

With the possible exception of the high gods, none of these spiritual beings was immortal. Nor were they concerned with human virtue: like the ancestors of the Shang kings, the deities worshipped by commoners in the Zhou dynasty responded to sacrifices as an exchange of favors. Sacrifice, divination, and—when gods became troublesome—exorcism were the usual forms of interaction between humans and gods. These rituals performed by commoners were primarily directed toward the welfare of individuals and families, in contrast to the predominant concerns among the élite for affairs of state. And the similarities between gods and humans—especially their mortality—reveal at this very early stage in the history of Chinese religion a characteristic that is still prominent today: the lack of a sharp distinction between the spiritual and mundane worlds.

We should remember that the worldviews of the élite and the commoners were not radically distinct either. The panoply of spiritual beings was known to all, and to the extent that members of the élite had family roots in the agricultural tradition, they too engaged in the ritual forms of propitiation of and communication with the various gods, ghosts, and spirits. The religious worldview was a continuous whole, in which differences in emphasis corresponded to differences in the immediate concerns and interests of its participants.

Toward the end of the Western Zhou period a new class of intellectuals arose.[6] This new élite sub-class, which produced the texts that formed the foundations of the Classical tradition, differed from the ruling élite mainly in its interpretation of the Mandate of Heaven. In the late Western Zhou (late ninth–early eighth century B.C.E.), the intellectual élite increasingly focused on this abstract notion of a moral Heaven, now seen less as a doctrine of political legitimation than as a religious basis for a system of ethical thought and practice; while the ruling élite, finding that the need for legitimation of their military takeover of the Shang (now about 200 years in the past) was not as pressing as it had once been, concentrated on the older systems of worship of royal ancestors and spirits of nature. These two strands of élite culture were reunited only with the "victory" of Confucianism as the officially sponsored ideology of government in the Han dynasty.

The Classical Period | 3

The Zhou dynasty began to break down in 771 B.C.E., when the king was assassinated during an attack by non-Chinese nomads from west of the capital city of Chang'an, and the capital was moved eastward to Luoyang, in the heart of the Yellow River valley. These events began a period of increasingly bitter strife and conflict that was to last 500 years. Roughly the first half of this period is known as the "Spring and Autumn" period, named after the *Spring and Autumn Annals*, a chronicle covering the years 722–481 B.C.E., supposedly written by Confucius. The latter half, up to the eventual reunification by the Qin dynasty in 221 B.C.E., is aptly called the "Warring States" period.

As the power of the Zhou kings waned, many of their nominal "vassals"—the hereditary dukes or feudal lords of the major regions—waged war against the others for dominance. Commoners were repeatedly conscripted into various armies, playing havoc with local agricultural economies (not to mention social morale and family life) as able-bodied men were forcibly taken away from their fields. Gradually the most powerful states (as the former fiefdoms were now called) gobbled up the weaker ones, and during the final century or so of the Warring States period, some of the dukes began calling themselves kings (*wang*), the title previously reserved for the central Zhou monarch.

This time of social and political chaos was a fertile period in the history of Chinese religion and philosophy and produced the traditions that we associate with classical Chinese civilization. Confucianism and Daoism are the best-known and most influential of these traditions, but roughly half a dozen major schools of thought arose during this period.

The collapse of the Zhou system persuaded most intellectuals that there was a critical need for a new political and ideological foundation for the state. There were, essentially, two aspects to the intellectual problem posed by the Zhou breakdown: theoretical and practical. The theoretical problem stemmed from the doctrine of the Mandate of Heaven: if Heaven is (or has) a moral will, and if Heaven is able to influence human events by replacing evil rulers with good ones, how can such violence and suffering continue?[1] This question, and the related question of human nature, became central to the Confucian tradition by the end of the Zhou period.

The practical problem, which on the whole received more attention than the theoretical one, was simply: how are we to restore social and political order and harmony? What is the proper role of government in human life, and how should society and government be organized? How can rulers discharge their moral responsibilities to their people? How can they maintain their legitimacy in the light of the Mandate of Heaven?

This was the intellectual setting that gave rise to the "Period of the Hundred Philosophers," as the Eastern Zhou is sometimes called. Given the notion of Heaven as the source of moral authority and political legitimacy, these interlocking problems are clearly both religious and political in nature.

Classical Confucianism

Confucius

Confucius was born in 551 B.C.E. in the small state of Lu, near the present city of **Qufu**. His given name was Kong Qiu; the name by which he was commonly known as an adult was Kong Zhongni, although many called him by the honorific name Kongzi, or Master Kong. "Confucius" is a Latinized name invented by seventeenth-century Jesuit missionaries in China, based on another, very rarely used honorific name, Kongfuzi.

His family were relatively impoverished aristocracy, and Confucius became an itinerant teacher with about thirty close disciples. His goal was to become the trusted adviser of one of the kings who were vying to re-establish a unified China under their control. In this he was never successful. While he reportedly held one or two minor government positions, he completely failed in his lifelong attempt to gain the trust of a king who would re-establish the glory of the early

Zhou dynasty. Nevertheless, he apparently had the personal charisma or moral authority to make a deep impression on his followers and to establish a reputation as a wise teacher. Over the centuries after his death he gradually came to personify a system of thought and practice that became inextricable from Chinese culture.

The best record we have of Confucius' teachings is a collection of his sayings and conversations, known in Chinese as the **Lunyu** (Discussions and Sayings) and in English as the *Analects*. This began to be compiled by his students shortly after his death, based on their recollections of his oral teachings. Further records, many of them undoubtedly apocryphal, were added to the book over the next century or more. So while we cannot regard it as a completely accurate historical record, the *Analects* does represent what Chinese people for two millennia have considered to be the actual teachings of Confucius. It is through the *Analects* that Confucius' thought has exerted its influence on Chinese intellectual and religious history.

Confucius' solution to the theoretical and practical problems raised by the breakdown of Zhou authority was that peace could be restored by reviving the moral character or virtue (*de*) of the ruling class. He believed that it was to this inner moral character that Heaven responded, not to the outward show of ritual or the exercise of force. He believed that society could be transformed by the moral cultivation of those in power, because virtue has a natural transformative effect on others. The perfectibility of the individual and of society as a whole were reciprocal goals, for the moral perfection of the self required a morally supportive social environment, with stable and loving families, opportunities for education, and good rulers who served as models. Society as a whole could best be perfected from the top down, so it was important to establish a government staffed by virtuous men (women did not serve in government). For these reasons Confucius directed his teaching toward local rulers and men whose goal was to serve in government. Literacy was a major component of the moral cultivation that he taught, and so he did not bring his message directly to the masses, the great majority of whom were illiterate. In later centuries, however, Confucian teachings would "trickle down" to all levels of society through the educational system.

A useful way of understanding Confucius' teaching in its intellectual context is to examine some key words that he redefined. The three most central of these are **ren** (humanity), **li** (ritual propriety), and **junzi** (superior person).

HUMANITY (REN) Before Confucius' time *ren* meant something like kindness, generosity, or benevolence, in particular that of a social superior to someone of lower social status. In Confucius' teaching it became the "cardinal virtue," and is best translated as "humanity." *Ren* is the perfection of what it means to be human, and in fact has the same dual connotation as "humanity": it is humaneness, or loving-kindness toward other beings, and it is also the essential characteristic of the human species. So for Confucius, to be human is to be humane.

But what does being humane entail? The closest we find to a definition of *ren* in the *Analects* is this: "Fan Chi asked about *ren*. The Master said, 'Love others'" (12:22). Most of the discussions of *ren* in the *Analects* are illustrations rather than definitions. The humane person, in addition to loving others, is "filial" (*xiao*) or respectful to parents and elders (1:2); respectful, reverent, loyal (13:19), strong, resolute, frugal, reticent (13:27), and trustworthy (17:6). And a humane person, knowing that to be human is to be humane, will choose death rather than forsake *ren* (15:9).

Humanity begins with a child's natural feelings of love and respect for its parents and the sense of self-worth or integrity that a well-loved and well-socialized person naturally develops by adulthood (1:1 and 1:2). The crucial moral step comes when one extends that inner sense of self-worth to others, in the form of love, concern, and correct behavior. "As for humaneness—you want to establish yourself, then help others to establish themselves. You want to develop yourself, then help others to develop themselves" (6:28/30).[2] This is called reciprocity (*shu*), which is also defined in terms of the Confucian Golden Rule: "What you would not want for yourself, do not do to others" (15:23/24).

RITUAL PROPRIETY (*LI*) *Li* originally referred to the ritual of sacrifice to gods or ancestors. By the time of Confucius its extended meaning was the attitude of reverence and respect, and the proper behavior that this implied, when one was performing such a ritual. But Confucius extended the meaning yet further. For him it was the proper mode of behavior in every situation, behavior that genuinely reflected the moral character of a humane person. Ritual behavior is empty and meaningless without *ren*: "If one is human yet not humane—what can one have to do with rites?" (3:3). But conversely, humanity *must* be expressed in proper social behavior: "Through mastering oneself and returning to ritual one becomes humane" (12:1).

Confucius had a very broad conception of the place of ritual in human life. Every aspect of life, he believed, should be carefully shaped according to patterns that express human values. In this sense a Confucian life becomes a continuing ceremony, symbolizing reverence for human culture and the uniquely human capacity for moral perfection. That Confucian ritual does not mean simply formal ceremony is expressed in the *Analects* by one of Confucius' disciples:

> There are three things that a gentleman [*junzi*, superior
> person], in following the Way, places above all the rest: from
> every attitude, every gesture that he employs he must
> remove all trace of violence or arrogance; every look that he
> composes in his face must betoken good faith; from every
> word that he utters, from every intonation, he must remove
> all trace of coarseness or impropriety. As to the ordering of
> ritual vessels and the like, there are those whose business it
> is to attend to such matters. (8:4)[3]

This comment clearly distinguishes the Confucian idea of *li* from the notion of going through the ritually correct motions without an inner sense of seriousness and good will. This reflects the "ethical revolution" that Confucius brought about in ancient China. Whereas the rituals of the Shang and early Zhou were deemed to be effective only if they were performed according to the correct procedures, Confucius gave ritual, for the first time, a moral basis.

THE SUPERIOR PERSON (*JUNZI*)   The original meaning of *junzi* was "son of a noble," referring to hereditary aristocracy. Confucius, however, understood true nobility in terms of moral character rather than genetic pedigree. In Confucian thought the *junzi* is a person who is dedicated to becoming a humane (*ren*) person. "Self-cultivation" (14:42) best characterizes the *junzi*, and is a process that requires constant self-examination (1:4, 4:17, 5:27, 9:24, 12:4, 15:21). For example:

> The Master said, "Walking along with three people, my teacher
> is sure to be among them. I choose what is good in them and
> follow it and what is not good and change it [in myself]." (7:21/22)

Another attribute of the superior person is a love of learning (***xue***). Although Confucius himself would not admit to being a fully humane person, he did take credit on this score:

> The Master said, "In a town of ten households, there must
> certainly be those as loyal and trustworthy as I, but none
> who cares as much about learning as I do." (5:27)

Learning for Confucians implies both self-cultivation and "study"
in a narrower sense. The object of such study in Confucius' time
was the cultural tradition handed down from the past. Confucius, again
characterizing himself, says, "I transmit but do not create; I trust and
love antiquity" (7:1). He believed that the Way of Heaven (***tiandao***) had been successfully put into practice during the time of the
early Zhou kings and had fallen into disuse. But that Way was preserved in the written records of those times and in other aspects of
the cultural tradition, such as the arts. Thus the learning of a superior person required studying certain written texts and learning ritual,
music, and literature. Chief among the written texts were the "Five
Classics" (***wu jing***).

The first of these is the ***Yijing***, or *Classic of Change*, a manual
of divination attributed to the primordial mythic culture-hero Fuxi,
incorporating later texts attributed to King Wen and the Duke of Zhou,
revered founders of the Zhou dynasty, and further explanatory
texts attributed to Confucius. These reputed origins gave the *Classic of Change* tremendous authority, and it was considered the earliest
and most profound expression of the Confucian Dao. The second text,
the ***Shijing***, or *Classic of Odes* (or *Songs*, or *Poetry*), allegedly edited
by Confucius, is a collection of poems or songs, including both popular folk songs and aristocratic hymns celebrating dynastic founders
and heroes. The third text, the ***Shujing***, or *Classic of Documents*,
purports to be a collection of official statements and documents from
the Xia, Shang, and early Zhou dynasties. It contains some of the earliest Chinese myths—stories concerning the ancient sage-kings
Yao, Shun, and Yu, who symbolize such fundamental Confucian
values as filiality and government by meritocracy. The fourth text, the
Qunqiu, or *Spring and Autumn (Annals)*, attributed to Confucius,
is a chronology of political events in the state of Lu, his home state.
The final classic comprised three works (the *Yili*, *Zhouli*, and ***Liji***),
describing the formal rituals of the early Zhou courts as well as the
modes of behavior, customs, dress, and other aspects of the lives of
the sage-kings—mostly reconstructed by much later writers.

These texts constituted the first Confucian canon, or body of sacred texts, and the original curriculum of Confucian education. They came to represent, at least for the ruling élite, the ideas, customs, and history of the virtuous founders of the Zhou. The culture (*wen*) they created—or the idealized picture of it in the texts—was the model human society that Confucians strove to achieve.

GOVERNING BY VIRTUE (*DE*) The purpose of government in Confucian thought is to function as a positive transformative force in society, to create a social environment that maximizes the likelihood that individuals will attend to and put into practice the will of Heaven, resulting in a state of order and harmony. Government is thus a religious issue in Confucianism. Confucius' theory of government is based on the notion of *de*, virtue or moral power: the power to influence others by setting a moral example. For example:

> The Master said, "Lead them by means of regulations and keep order among them through punishments, and the people will evade them and will lack any sense of shame [or self-respect]. Lead them through moral force (*de*) and keep order among them through rites (*li*), and they will have a sense of shame and will also correct themselves." (2:3)

The idea is that people are naturally attracted to a moral ruler, and will follow his example without being coerced. Indeed, this kind of influence—moral force—is ultimately more effective than political or legal coercion: when people are inspired by the ruler's good example there is less need for intrusive laws and harsh punishments.

The idea that people are naturally attracted to goodness is an incipient theory of human nature. As Confucius says in a conversation with a government official,

> If you, sir, want goodness, the people will be good. The virtue of the noble person (*junzi*) is like the wind, and the virtue of small people is like grass. When the wind blows over the grass, the grass must bend. (12:19)

This, of course, is an idealized picture of a perfect society, but the general theory of government as more than a necessary evil, as a force for moral good, still has relevance today.

The followers of Confucius came to be known as *ru* or "scholars," signifying their relationship with the arts and classics: they were in a sense custodians of and experts in the literate cultural tradition (*wen*), especially in the areas of court ritual and protocol. For them, the culture of the early Zhou kings, as recorded in the classics, would provide the moral map leading to the ultimate perfection of individuals and society—the coordinate goals of the Confucian Way.

Mencius

Confucius was a teacher rather than a philosopher: he generally stated his views without rational argumentation or defense. The first true Confucian philosopher—or the first to leave a written record—was Mencius (fourth century B.C.E.). His real name was Meng Ke, and he is generally called Mengzi, or Master Meng. He is the only other Chinese thinker whose Jesuit, Latinized name is still used. He was born roughly a century after Confucius died, and may have been a disciple of Confucius' grandson. Unlike Confucius, Mencius did become adviser to several local rulers, although none of them put his ideas into practice. The book containing his conversations, called simply the *Mencius* (*Mengzi*), was probably compiled from nearly verbatim notes by his students. It is more consistent and more reliable than the *Analects* and it contains extended discussions in which Mencius fully develops his positions and defends them against those of other philosophers.

The two major, interconnected themes of the *Mencius* are humane government (**ren zheng**) and human nature (**ren xing**). Mencius' theory of human nature became the foundation upon which the Confucian tradition rested after the eleventh century. Confucius had made only scant suggestions concerning human nature, mostly by implication. The term **xing**, meaning the nature of a thing, was not a major part of the philosophical lexicon in Confucius' time. A century later, though, it had become a hot topic of philosophical debate.

HUMANE GOVERNMENT Mencius argues that the ruler's first responsibility is to ensure that his people can feed, clothe, and house themselves. Only then can he expect them to serve in the army, and only then can he encourage them to cultivate themselves morally (1A:7). The ruler should treat his subjects like himself, allowing them to enjoy what he enjoys (1B:5), and thereby act as "father and mother to the people" (1B:7).

This theory is based on Confucius' idea that virtue is more effective than force in governing a state. The difference between the use of force and the use of virtue defined, for Mencius, the difference between the way of the "despot" and the way of the "true king" (2A:3). The despot—by which Mencius meant the majority of the rulers of the Warring States—may achieve superficial benefits for his people, but the true king serves both their material and their spiritual needs. Government by moral example works best because human beings are naturally attracted to the good, and they are attracted to the good because exposure to moral examples has a pleasurable, nourishing effect on their own inherently good natures. The satisfaction of this innate moral nature constitutes a self-realization that grounds human beings in the larger cosmos:

> All the ten thousand things are complete in me. To turn within to examine oneself and find that one is authentic [real, genuine]—there is no greater joy than this. (7A:4)

This also suggests a mystical dimension to Mencius' thought—a sense of identity with the cosmos that fully actualizes one's Heaven-given moral nature. This reveals the religious dimension of Confucian thought—a religious dimension that is realized only in the concrete world of social activity.

HUMAN NATURE Mencius believed that human nature (*xing*) is inherently good, that moral inclinations are natural and unique to human beings. He explains this in what became one of the most important and well-known passages in Chinese philosophical literature:

> Here is why I say that all human beings have a mind that commiserates with others. Now, if anyone were suddenly to see a child about to fall into a well, his mind would always [in all cases] be filled with alarm, distress, pity, and compassion. [This][4] is not because he would use the opportunity to ingratiate himself with the child's parents, nor because he would seek commendation from neighbors and friends, nor because he would hate the adverse reputation. From this it may be seen that one who lacks a mind that feels pity and compassion would not be human; one who lacks a mind that feels shame and aversion would not be human; one who lacks a mind that feels mod-

esty and compliance would not be human; and one who lacks a mind that knows right and wrong would not be human.

The mind's feeling of pity and compassion is the beginning of humaneness (*ren*); the mind's feeling of shame and aversion is the beginning of rightness (*yi*); the mind's feeling of modesty and compliance is the beginning of propriety (*li*); and the mind's sense of right and wrong is the beginning of wisdom (*zhi*). Human beings have these four beginnings just as they have four limbs. (2A:6)

Mencius believed that reflecting on this example would convince anyone that no human being could fail to react in some way to the sight of a child falling into a well. Even the twinge of guilt (or pleasure) that might be felt by a cruel person choosing to ignore the child would demonstrate that there is some innate sense of compassion or knowledge of right and wrong within us all. His statement that one lacking such feelings would not be human should be taken to mean that it is inconceivable that any human being could lack them.

The "four beginnings"—*ren, yi, li,* and *zhi*—are the innate sources of morality, according to Mencius' theory. But they are only beginnings, or "seeds," which need to be cultivated in order to become the full-fledged virtues of humanity, rightness, ritual propriety, and wisdom. Until then they are merely "feelings" or "dispositions" (**qing**). Thus Mencius' theory of the goodness of human nature is really a theory of potential goodness:

> As far as the natural tendencies (*qing*) are concerned, it is possible for one to do good; this is what I mean by being good. If one does what is not good, that is not the fault of one's capacities. (6A:6)

But potentiality is more than mere possibility. The feelings described by the "four beginnings" represent the existing capacities to become humane, etc. They are as natural and concrete as our four limbs, and are unique to the human species. Human nature, then, is not a static essence; it is the natural course of human development, distinguished from that of other animals by the actualization of our moral potential. In cultivating our moral capacities we become fully human.

Why, then, do people do evil things? Mencius says that the difference between good and bad people is simply that the former use their minds. "By thinking, one gets it; by not thinking, one fails to get it" (6A:15). "It" is the importance of recognizing one's own moral potential and cultivating it. But then why do some people use their minds in this way while others do not? Ultimately, the answer is environment. All people have the capacity to become good, but that process requires active cultivation in an environment in which moral models are available for emulation, an environment in which acquiring the basic necessities of life does not take up all one's time and energy, and a childhood environment in which one's sense of self-worth is nourished by love. Mencius uses biological analogies to make this point. In his famous Ox Mountain allegory (6A:8), he compares humans who have become bad to a naturally wooded mountain that has become denuded. Even though shoots and sprouts are constantly coming up from the soil, the grazing of cattle and the logging of woodsmen result in a deforested mountain. Likewise, a person's innately good nature can wither if it is not "preserved and nourished."

Thus Mencius' solution to what we call the "nature/nurture" controversy is that all human beings are good by nature: "The sage and we are the same in kind" (6A:7). It is because of their nurturance that some people are good and others bad. This is consistent with Confucius' enigmatic saying, "By nature close together; in practice far apart" (*Analects* 17:2). External nurturance, or environment, plays a role in this system analogous to the role of grace in Christian theology. In Christian thought, we are by nature sinful, and it is only God's free gift, the redemption of sin—which we do not deserve on our own merits—that saves us. In Mencian thought the premise is exactly the opposite: we are by nature good, but something external is still required to actualize that potential.

Mencius' position on the problem of the existence of evil emphasizes the importance of family life and education. The family is, in fact, our first classroom. There we are exposed to our first moral models or exemplary teachers; there our innate tendencies to love others and respect those above us (our parents and other elders) take form. This is why filiality (*xiao*) is said, in the *Analects*, to be the "root of the Way" (1:2). Later (if one is fortunate) education continues outside the family. (In ancient China, girls were generally not given a formal education, and if they learned to read and write at all it was in the home.) Education exposes one not only to exemplary teachers, who have the same transforming effect as virtuous rulers, but also to the supreme examples of the sages, recorded in the classics.

To understand fully the religious aspect of Mencian Confucianism, it is helpful to agree on a definition of religion. One of the more concise and useful of the many definitions that have been proposed is that of the late scholar of Buddhism Frederick Streng, who proposed that religion is a "means of ultimate transformation."[5] By "ultimate" he meant that the goal of religious life is defined in terms of whatever the tradition in question believes to be absolute or unconditioned—such as God in the biblical traditions.

Becoming a sage in Confucianism is obviously a transformation, but is it an ultimate transformation? Mencius says,

> To fully develop one's mind is to know one's nature. To know one's nature is to know Heaven. Preserving one's mind and nourishing one's nature is how one serves Heaven. (7A:1)[6]

Heaven (*tian*) is the Confucian symbol of ultimacy, that which is unconditioned. Self-knowledge is equivalent to knowing and serving Heaven because the goodness of human nature is given by Heaven. Confucius had said, "Heaven has given birth to the virtue that is in me" (*Analects* 7:22/21). The early Confucian text *Centrality and Commonality* (**Zhongyong**), which is closely associated with the Mencian line of Confucian thought, begins with the line "What Heaven has endowed is called the nature."[7] In other words, self-cultivation is not only self-realization; it is realizing (making real) the moral potential of the cosmos. Only human beings can do this. Human beings are therefore "co-creators" of the cosmos. As the *Centrality and Commonality* says,

> Only that one in the world who is most perfectly authentic is able to give full development to his nature. Being able to give full development to his nature, he is able to give full development to the nature of other human beings and, being able to give full development to the nature of other human beings, he is able to give full development to the natures of other living things. Being able to give full development to the natures of other living things, he can assist in the transforming and nourishing powers of Heaven and Earth; being able to assist in the transforming and nourishing powers of Heaven and Earth, he can form a triad with Heaven and Earth.[8]

This passage is probably the best expression in the classical Confucian literature of the religious dimension of Confucian self-cultivation. And as we shall see, it has parallels in both Buddhism and Daoism.

Xunzi

The Mencian interpretation of the Confucian tradition eventually became the orthodox one, but not until the Song dynasty (960–1279). Other Confucian thinkers were influential from the end of the classical period at least through the Han dynasty (206 B.C.E.–220 C.E.). Xunzi (Master Xun), or Xun Qing, was probably born a few years before Mencius died, and lived roughly until the time that the Qin dynasty reunited China in 221 B.C.E. He is best known for his claim that "human nature is evil," directly contradicting Mencius. But his dispute with Mencius is more about the meaning of the term "nature" (*xing*) than about the constitution of the human personality. Xunzi claims that any trait that must be cultivated cannot be the nature of a thing; the nature of a thing must be something that appears spontaneously, without any training. By these criteria, he says, Mencius was wrong, because his theory was really about the moral potential that is innate to human beings, as we have seen.

More significantly, Xunzi agrees that all people have the potential to become sages, but he is more conscious of the difficulties and does not allow for the possibility of doing this by self-reflection. We need the external influence of the sages of the past, and especially the character-molding influence of the rituals that they devised. So for Xunzi, becoming a sage is a matter of transformation, while for Mencius it is a matter of cultivation or development.

Xunzi also disagrees with the Confucian assumption that Heaven has a moral will. For him, Heaven is simply the natural world, which has no moral character at all. Thus human beings should focus attention on the human, social realm, because any good that can come about can only be the product of our deliberate actions (*wei*). In this respect he pushes Confucius' thinking to a logical conclusion that Confucius himself would probably not have accepted.

Classical Daoism

The term "classical Daoism" refers to what is often called "philosophical Daoism," as opposed to "religious Daoism." This distinction, in turn, is based on the Chinese terms **Daojia** (School of the Way) and **Daojiao** (Teaching of the Way). *Daojia* has been used for many centuries to refer mainly to the Daoist classics *Daodejing* (Classic of the Way and its Power) and *Zhuangzi* (named after its main author, Master Zhuang). *Daojiao* refers to the fully developed religion of Daoism, which, most scholars agree, began in the second century C.E. In this chapter we will be looking only at classical Daoism, which evolved at roughly the same time as classical Confucianism and in dialogue with it.

Confucianism and Daoism have much in common. They both emphasize the goal of establishing a harmony of heaven, earth, and humanity. They both display a kind of thinking known as organicism, which defines things by their functional relationships to larger wholes (like organs in organisms). And they both arose in the Warring States period as proposed solutions to the social and political chaos then gripping China.

For a worldview in which the ideal state is a harmony of heaven, earth, and humanity, the collapse of the political order indicates that something is wrong in the cosmos as a whole. The Confucian response, as we have seen, was that social and political order (and hence cosmic order) could be restored by reviving the moral character of the ruling class: fix society and the cosmic order will be restored. The early Daoists had a different diagnosis, and of course a different prescription. In their view, what had been lost was not the enlightened social and governmental institutions of the ancient kings, but rather the harmony between human society and the natural world. The problem, according to them, concerned human beings' relationship with nature, not their relationship with each other. They argued that human beings should model their behavior on nature, not on an earlier society. For the Daoists, human beings are *natural* beings, and society is a corrupting influence.

Laozi

According to tradition, Laozi was an older contemporary of Confucius, possibly named Li Er (and also called Lao Dan, or Old Dan), who worked as chief librarian of the Zhou royal house. Near the end of his life, according to the stories, Laozi left the Zhou kingdom, passing through the Jade Gate of the Western Pass outside the capital city of Chang'an. The gatekeeper, knowing his reputation as a wise man, asked him to write something before he left, and Laozi wrote down

Laozi and Confucius, in an eighteenth-century silk painting by Wang Shugu. Confucius is depicted holding a baby to suggest the importance of family and progeny in the Confucian tradition.

the text we know as the *Laozi*, or *Daodejing* (Classic of the Way and its Power). It is a short text consisting of approximately 5000 words, in eighty-one brief chapters. Much of it is in poetic form.

The modern view is that there is no historical information whatsoever about the author of the *Laozi*. The text itself took shape over a century or more—probably from a core of orally transmitted sayings—by about the third century B.C.E. Although there is some internal consistency in it, the text is clearly the product of several authors. The name "Laozi," after all, is not actually a name: it simply means "Old Master," or perhaps "Old Masters." Nevertheless, for convenience we will refer to Laozi as a person, albeit a historical fiction.

The central concept of the *Laozi* is the Dao, the "way" or "path." The term is fundamental to both Confucianism and Daoism, but each school understands it differently. In the *Laozi* there are essentially two sets of meanings of Dao: Dao as the Way of nature, and Dao as a Way of life. The central message of the *Laozi* is that to live a meaningful, fulfilled human life, one's way of life should be modeled after the Way of nature.

WAY OF NATURE The *Laozi* begins with one of the most quoted and most enigmatic statements in religious literature:

> The Way that can be spoken of is not the constant Way;
> The name that can be named is not the constant name.
> The nameless is the beginning of Heaven and Earth;
> The named is the mother of all things.

There are many ways to interpret this verse, and many ways to translate it, but by "constant Way" Laozi probably means the true Dao, the ultimate reality. Thus the first line means that the ultimate truth is ineffable, beyond the reach of language and conceptual thinking. Anything that we can clearly attach a name to is not the Way and has only a relative existence. But behind all relative things is a nameless reality that is the absolute, unconditioned origin of the cosmos:

> There is a thing confusedly formed, born before Heaven and Earth.
> Silent and void it stands alone and does not change,
> Goes round and does not weary.
> It is capable of being the mother of the world.
> I know not its name so I style it "the Way." (25)[9]

Perhaps reflecting the multiple authorship of the *Laozi*, this unnameable "thing"—the Dao—is sometimes referred to as "nothing," or as that which precedes the universe:

> The myriad creatures in the world are born from Something,
> And Something from Nothing. (40)

The Way begets one; one begets two; two begets three; three begets the myriad creatures. (42)[10]

The Dao is also described as being empty or vacuous:

Between Heaven and Earth—how like a bellows!
Vacuous but inexhaustible, moving and producing ever more. (5)[11]

Thirty spokes conjoin in one hub;
there being nothing in between, the cart is useful.
Clay is molded to form a vessel;
there being nothing inside, the vessel is useful.
…
Thus, with something one gets advantage,
While with nothing one gets usefulness. (11)

The point here is that it is the emptiness at the hub of a wheel (where the axle fits) and inside a bowl that makes these objects useful; emptiness is their virtue. This virtue or potential is *de* (as in the title *Daodejing*), which we saw earlier as the Confucian concept of moral virtue or moral potential. But in Daoist usage, *de* is not moral power, it is the power to do whatever a thing does. It is also symbolized in the *Laozi* by the image of an uncarved block of wood (15, 28, 32, 37, 57), which is simple, whole, and unmanipulated by human action, yet has unlimited potential.

One of the apparent contradictions in the *Laozi* is that there are some passages that say that the Way is characterized by change (e.g. ch. 40) and others that state or imply that the Way is unchanging (e.g. ch. 1). Of course, we could simply attribute these inconsistencies to multiple authorship, but there may also be some coherence to them. The physical world is dynamically changing, yet there are patterns to that change. The Dao is the ultimate pattern, the ultimate source of order and hence the ultimate origin of the cosmos, a transcendent reality, beyond the world of experience. Yet the Dao is also the sum total of all changing phenomena, and in that sense it is immanent (ever present). These two meanings of Dao are referred to in chapter 1:

The Way that can be spoken of is not the constant Way;
The name that can be named is not the constant name.

The nameless is the beginning of Heaven and Earth;
The named is the mother of all things.

Thus be constantly without desire, so as to observe its subtlety,
And constantly have desire, so as to observe its outcome.

These two have the same origin, but are named differently.
Both may be called mysterious.
Mysterious and still more mysterious,
The gateway of all subtleties!

According to this interpretation, the "nameless" is the Dao as the ultimate pattern and source of all changing phenomena, the constant Way, beyond our ability to conceive, while the "named" is the Dao as the process of change itself, the actual world of phenomena that we experience cognitively and express in language. Most importantly, these two are not separate realms of being, but two aspects of one reality. The ultimate source of meaning is not to be found outside the world of concrete, changing phenomena, but within it. This insight was later shared by both Chinese Buddhism and Neo-Confucianism.

WAY OF LIFE The interpretation of the Dao as the Way of nature has implications for how we should live, as individuals and as a society. The goal of individual life, according to the *Laozi*, is to live the longest possible natural life by living in harmony with one's social and natural environment. In terms of government—we must not forget that the political situation was part of the *raison d'être* of this text—the goal was to restore political unity and harmony by the least coercive means possible. The figure of the sage (**sheng**) represented the achievement of both of these goals:

Therefore the sage says:
I do nothing (*wuwei*), and the people are transformed by themselves.
I value tranquillity, and the people become correct by themselves.
I take no action (*wushi*), and the people become prosperous by themselves.
I have no desires, and the people of themselves become like uncarved wood. (57)

"Doing nothing" or "non-action" (**wuwei**) is probably the *Laozi*'s most important prescription both for living a meaningful life as an individual and for leading a government. However, it does not mean literally doing nothing: it means we should refrain from unnatural action, or action based on conscious, intentional thinking. Instead, we should allow ourselves to act spontaneously, reacting intuitively to each particular situation.

There are three reasons for favoring spontaneity over conscious activity. First, the fact that the Dao is ineffable means that we should not trust our cognitive capacity to respond appropriately to the constantly changing configuration of events. Second, if we are to emulate the way the natural world operates, we must acknowledge that nature does not act with conscious deliberation:

> Man models himself on earth,
> Earth on heaven,
> Heaven on the way,
> And the way on that which is naturally so. (25)

"That which is naturally so" is the Chinese compound **ziran**, which literally means "self-so." It means that the Dao is what it is in and of itself; it is not dependent on anything else. *Ziran* means both "natural" and "spontaneous"; it is a positive counterpart to the negative term *wuwei*.

Third, what we learn by observing nature is that spontaneous action is ultimately more effective than planned action. In two places in the *Laozi* we find the deliberately paradoxical statement,

> By doing nothing (*wuwei*), nothing is left undone. (37, 48)

The text contains numerous illustrations of the principle that goal-directed action is ultimately self-defeating, and that to be effective it is best not actively to pursue a goal. Paradoxes such as this recur throughout the *Laozi*, illustrating the limitations of logical, discursive thought. They emphasize the need to use language creatively, since reality does not exactly fit our neat conceptual and linguistic categories:

> Be bent so as to become whole,
> Be crooked so as to become straight,

> Be empty so as to become full,
> Be worn so as to become new. (22)

Acting contrary to the common-sense approach of identifying a goal and pursuing it leads to less conflict, more contentment, and longer life. Another way of maximizing longevity, closely related to *wuwei*, is to follow a path of yielding and humility. This is often expressed by imagery concerned with water and valleys, and alluding to "feminine" virtues:

> The spirit of the valley does not die.
> It is called the mysterious female.
> The gate of the mysterious female
> Is called the root of Heaven and Earth.
> Being continuous, it is as if it existed always.
> Being used, it is still not exhausted. (6)

> In the world there is nothing more submissive and weak than water. Yet for attacking that which is hard and strong nothing can surpass it. (78, cf. 43)

> Therefore a weapon that is strong will not vanquish;
> A tree that is strong will suffer the axe.
> The strong and big takes the lower position,
> The supple and weak takes the higher position. (76)

By being still and quiet, by being content with what one has, and by adapting spontaneously and naturally to one's circumstances rather than acting in accordance with preconceived goals, an ordinary person can live a full and long life, and a ruler can (paradoxically) achieve his goal of restoring harmony to his realm.

The social goal envisaged by the *Laozi* is portrayed in chapter 80:

> Let the state be small and the people be few.
> There may be ten or even a hundred times as many implements, but they should not be used.
> Let the people, regarding death as a weighty matter, not travel far.
> Though they have boats and carriages, none shall ride in them.
> Though they have armor and weapons, none shall display them.

> Let the people return once more to the use of knotted ropes [for
> record-keeping].
> Let them savor their food and find beauty in their clothing, peace
> in their dwellings, and joy in their customs.
> Though neighboring states are within sight of one another, and
> the sound of cocks and dogs is audible from one to the other,
> People will reach old age and death and yet not visit one another.

This is a utopian vision of a small-scale, self-sufficient, low-tech
society, whose people are happy with what they have and not dri-
ven to expand or explore. While it may seem too simple for many
of us today, in comparison with the social and political chaos and violence of the Warring States period it must have seemed attractive
indeed.

It was mentioned earlier that classical Confucianism and classical Daoism developed in dialogue with each other. We see some of
that in the *Laozi*, in the form of criticism of many basic Confucian
ideas:

> When the great Way declined, there were humaneness and
> rightness.
> When intelligence and wisdom emerged, there was great
> artifice. (18)

> Do away with sageliness, discard knowledge,
> And the people will benefit a hundredfold.
> Do away with humaneness, discard rightness,
> And the people will once more be filial and loving. (19)

All of these terms are key Confucian concepts, well known by the time
the *Laozi* was compiled. Laozi calls them all "artifice" (*wei*), which
means something like "man-made." For Xunzi this same term suggests human creativity, but for Laozi it simply means "artificial."

Like Confucianism, classical Daoism has two interdependent
goals. For society the goal is to live in peaceful, small-scale communities, ruled with a light touch by sages who practice government
by "non-action." For the individual it is to live the longest possible
natural life by being in harmony with nature and minimizing conflict.
And there are vague hints in the *Laozi* that there were meditative
practices that might help people achieve those goals.

In preserving the soul and embracing the One, can you avoid
departing from them?
In concentrating your *qi* and arriving at utmost weakness,
can you be like an infant? (10)

Some scholars argue that the *Laozi* is just part of a much richer
tradition of contemporary religious thought and practice, but this
is highly speculative.[12] Was Daoism in the Warring States period a full-
fledged religion, or was it merely a current of intellectual thought?
Scholars are not able yet to answer this question, but it seems appro-
priate that, at least for now, Daoism's origins are shrouded in mystery.

Zhuangzi

Unlike Laozi, Zhuang Zhou, known as Zhuangzi (Master Zhuang),
seems to have been a real person who was a contemporary of Mencius
in the fourth century B.C.E. The text known by his name is one of
the masterpieces of classical Chinese literature. It is elegant, humorous, and philosophically rich. Of the thirty-three chapters that we
have today, only the first seven are considered to be by Zhuangzi himself, although others are probably by close disciples and certainly
reflect his thought, if not the brilliance of his writing. Still others
are only peripherally related to Zhuangzi's thought.

The *Zhuangzi* differs from the *Laozi* in several respects. Unlike
the majority of Warring States philosophical works, it does not
have a political focus but instead focuses entirely on how the individual can live a meaningful life in harmony with the Dao. Zhuangzi's
sage is a free spirit, but less mysterious and more earthy than Laozi's,
seeking less to preserve life than to appreciate it to the full. One of
Zhuangzi's frequently used metaphors is that of "free and easy wandering"—the title of the first chapter. This symbolizes freedom
from convention and social structure; freedom from preconceived categories of value, usefulness, and beauty; and freedom from the fear of
death rather than a concern with lengthening life. Zhuangzi seems to
have a deeper appreciation of human creativity—most of the people he depicts as being in tune with the Way are artists or craftsmen—and
he sees the Dao as the beginningless and endless process of transformation, not as the ultimate origin of Heaven and Earth.

As with Laozi, we can usefully approach Zhuangzi's thought from
the dual perspectives of his view of the Way of nature and his view of the
Way of life, noting the implications that the former has for the latter.

WAY OF NATURE Transformation (***hua***) is the key concept in Zhuangzi's view of the natural world. The cosmos is in constant flux, and the Dao is the sum total of all natural processes. Zhuangzi emphatically denies that reality is to be found anywhere outside the phenomenal world of change:

> Does heaven revolve? Does the earth stand still?
> Do the sun and moon jockey for position?
> Who controls all of this? Who unfolds all of this? Who ties it all together?
> Who dwells in inactivity, yet impels things on their course?
> May it be that there are levers and threads that drive them inexorably?
> Or may it be that they just keep turning and are unable to stop by themselves?[13]

The answer to the rhetorical questions posed by Zhuangzi in this passage is that there is no external directing force. Things transform themselves; the principle of movement or change is inherent within them:

> The life of things is like the cantering and galloping of a horse—
> They are transformed with each movement, they change with each moment.
> What are you to do? What are you not to do?
> Just let things evolve by themselves [*zihua*, self-transformation].[14]

The uncreated nature of the cosmos is made even more explicit by one of the earliest authoritative commentators on the *Zhuangzi*, Guo Xiang (d. 312 C.E.):

> Therefore before we can talk about creation, we must understand the fact that all things materialize by themselves. If we go through the entire realm of existence, we shall see that there is nothing, not even the penumbra, that does not transform itself beyond the phenomenal world. Hence everything creates itself without the direction of any Creator.[15]

WAY OF LIFE Given this view of the external world, what ways of thinking are best suited to guide a person through life? Zhuangzi proposes
an emotional response and an intellectual response to this question.

On the emotional level, Zhuangzi argues for equanimity in the
face of change. One should not sorrow over the transience of things;
rather, one should delight in their participation in the universal process
of transformation. Zhuangzi tells a story of four friends, one of
whom suddenly becomes crippled and disfigured. When asked if he
resents it, he says he does not: he actually looks forward to the new
uses that his transformed body might be good for. He continues,

> Furthermore, what we attain is due to timeliness and what
> we lose is the result of compliance. If we repose in timeliness
> and dwell in compliance, sorrow and joy cannot affect us.
> This is what the ancients called "emancipation."

To "repose in timeliness and dwell in compliance" is to adapt constantly to one's changing circumstances.

Suddenly one of the other friends falls ill and is about to die.
His family gather around him weeping. One of his friends says,

> "Shush! Go away! Do not disturb transformation!" Then,
> leaning against the door, he spoke to Sir Come [his dying
> friend]: "Great is the Transforming Creator! What next will
> he make of you? Where will he send you? Will he turn you
> into a rat's liver? Will he turn you into a bug's leg?"

> ... [Sir Come replies:] "The Great Clod burdens me with
> form, toils me through life, eases me in old age, rests me in
> death. Thus, that which makes my life good is also that
> which makes my death good."[16]

One of the most famous stories depicts Zhuangzi's reactions to his
wife's death:

> Master Zhuang's wife died. When Master Hui went to offer his
> condolences, he found Master Zhuang lolling on the floor
> with his legs sprawled out, beating a basin and singing.

> "She lived together with you," said Master Hui, "raised your

children, grew old, and died. It's enough that you do not wail
for her, but isn't it a bit much for you to be beating on a basin
and singing?"

"Not so," said Master Zhuang. "When she first died, how
could I of all people not be melancholy? But I reflected on
her beginning and realized that originally she was unborn.
Not only was she unborn, originally she had no form. Not
only did she have no form, originally she had no vital breath
[qi]. Intermingling with nebulousness and blurriness, a
transformation occurred and there was form; the form was
transformed and there was birth; now there has been
another transformation and she is dead. This is like the
progression of the four seasons—from spring to autumn,
from winter to summer. There she sleeps blissfully in an
enormous chamber. If I were to have followed her weeping
and wailing, I think it would have been out of keeping with
destiny [ming], so I stopped."[17]

If Zhuangzi appears a bit inhuman in his reaction to his wife's death,
we should notice that he overcomes his natural sadness by a process
of reflection in which he comes to see her life and her death as merely
parts of an ongoing process of transformation. Although he uses his
intellect to gain a broader perspective on his emotions, he does not
deny or repress his natural emotional response.

Zhuangzi's intellectual response to change and transformation is
based on a thoroughgoing critique of language and cognitive knowledge. All our linguistic and cognitive categories, all our views and
claims about the world, he says, are relative to particular perspectives:
"A way comes into being through our walking upon it; a thing is so
because people say that it is."[18] In this radically relativistic view, "one
is entitled to affirm or deny anything of anything."[19] Is there something objectively inherent in a road that makes it a road? Or is it
our use of it that makes it a road? If I dream I'm a butterfly, when I
wake up how do I know that I'm not a butterfly dreaming I'm human?[20]
Or even,

How do I know that love of life is not a delusion? How do I
know that fear of death is not like being a homeless waif who
does not know the way home?[21]

All judgments and claims are conditioned by the subject's perspective, and unless we can free ourselves from these limited perspectives we cannot regard any of our knowledge as true or unconditioned.

Such objective knowledge is attainable. Zhuangzi's term for it is "seeing things in the light of Heaven" or "lucidity" (**ming**, clarity):

> Where "this" and "that" cease to be opposites, there lies the pivot of the Way [*daoshu*]. Only when the pivot is located in the center of the circle of things can we respond to their infinite transformations. The transformations of "right" are infinite and so are the transformations of "wrong."Therefore, it is said that nothing is better for responding to them than lucidity.[22]

The perspective of the Dao is the broadest possible viewpoint, free from the limitations of one's own history, conditioning, and circumstances. The process by which Zhuangzi transcended the sorrow he felt for his wife's death is an example: he stepped further and further back from his own sense of loss to see her life and death as temporary phases in the universal process of change.

How can this be accomplished? Zhuangzi offers more concrete advice than Laozi, in a long dialogue between Confucius and his favorite disciple, Yan Hui. Confucius' advice to Yan Hui is to practice "fasting of the mind"(**xinzhai**):

> Make your will one! Don't listen with your ears, listen with your mind. No, don't listen with your mind, listen with your spirit (*qi*). Listening is limited to the ears, the mind is limited to recognition, but spirit is empty and waits on all things. The way gathers in emptiness alone. Emptiness (**xu**) is the fasting of the mind.[23]

Zhuangzi means that ordinary knowledge consists simply in recognizing experiences in terms of categories that one has previously learned. When something in the external world can be fitted into one of our mental cubbyholes, we place it there—whether it is a good fit or not. All of these mental categories, according to Zhuangzi, are learned and therefore conditional, perspectival, and limited. But

> The mind of the ultimate man functions like a mirror. It neither sends off nor welcomes; it responds but does not retain.[24]

The perfected person or the sage neither projects his mental categories onto the world nor retains images in his mind to function as preconceived categories for future acts of knowing. His mind is like a mirror rather than photographic film: it reflects just what is present at the moment. When the object of knowledge is gone, the mind retains no record of it that will color his view of the next object.

> Just ride along with things as you let your mind wander.
> Entrust yourself to inevitability and thereby nourish what is
> central. That's the ultimate course.[25]

By emptying the mind of all preconceived ideas and allowing the mind to respond to things as they are, we can see things from the perspective of the Dao (the "pivot of the Way"), a perspective that is unconditioned by our past learning and personal experience.

This does not mean making no distinctions at all; it means "sorting things out" according to the present situation, taking into account all the conditions of the present moment. It is an intuitive rather than intellectual kind of knowing: a spontaneous response to the changing pattern of events—in effect changing along with it—unmediated by cognitive processing:

> Craftsman Chui could draft as accurately freehand as if he
> were using compass and L-square because his fingers evolved
> [hua, transformed] with things and he did not calculate with
> his mind.[26]

"Fasting of the mind"—emptying the mind of preconceived categories and attending to the totality of what is actually present—can be achieved by "sitting and forgetting" (*zuowang*), a term that undoubtedly refers to a kind of meditation:

> Yan Hui said, "I smash up my limbs and body, drive out
> perception and intellect, cast off form, do away with
> understanding, and make myself identical with the Great
> Thoroughfare. This is what I mean by sitting down and
> forgetting everything."

> Confucius said, "If you're identical with it, you must have no
> more likes! If you've been transformed, you must have no

more constancy! So you really are a worthy man after all!
With your permission, I'd like to become your follower."[27]

Having no likes and no constancy means being in a state of fluid responsiveness and receptivity, not predisposed to filter reality through pre-learned categories that were not derived from the present set of circumstances.

To maintain one's authenticity or genuineness in the face of a world that is constantly changing, one must achieve this state of fluid responsiveness and be able to adapt to one's changing environment. A story in one of the later chapters of the *Zhuangzi* illustrates this nicely:

> Confucius was observing the cataract at Spinebridge where the water fell from a height of thirty fathoms and the mist swirled for forty tricents. No tortoise, alligator, fish, or turtle could swim there. Spotting an older man swimming in the water, Confucius thought that he must have suffered some misfortune and wished to die. So he had his disciples line up along the current to rescue the man. But after the man had gone several hundred yards he came out by himself. With disheveled hair, he was walking along singing and enjoying himself beneath the embankment.

> Confucius followed after the man and inquired of him, saying, "I thought you were a ghost, but when I looked more closely I saw that you are a man. May I ask if you have a special way for treading the water?"

> "No, I have no special way. I began with what was innate, grew up with my nature, and completed my destiny. I enter the very center of the whirlpools and emerge as a companion of the torrent. I follow along with the way of the water and do not impose myself on it. That's how I do my treading."[28]

As we might say today, Zhuangzi teaches us to "go with the flow."

The Han dynasty (206 B.C.E.–9 C.E. and 23–220) was the first great imperial period, lasting about 400 years (with a short interruption in the middle). To this day, "Han" is synonymous, in some ways, with "Chinese." From the fall of the Han in 220 C.E. to 589, China was ruled by a large number of regional kingdoms, but none was able to achieve  reunification until the short-lived Sui dynasty (589–618), immediately followed by the Tang (618–906). The period of disunity is known as the Six Dynasties period, or is divided into two periods: the Wei-Jin and the Northern and Southern dynasties.

Han-dynasty religious thought was syncretic, bringing together elements from various traditions, including an elaborate body of cosmological theory. Confucianism became the state religion in the second century B.C.E., Buddhism was introduced from India in the first century C.E., and organized Daoist religion began in the second century C.E. During the period of disunity that followed the Han dynasty, Confucianism declined and both Buddhism and Daoism flourished. The Sui and Tang dynasties saw the development of new, distinctly Chinese schools of Buddhism and new developments in the Daoist religion. During the later Tang the first stirrings of a Confucian revival appeared.

Cosmology and Popular Religion

A number of theories about how the world works, or how natural processes occur, were systematized during the Han. These theories became the foundations of Chinese scientific thought and certain aspects of religious thought. We shall examine them, briefly, in ascending order of complexity.

Dao, Change, and *Qi*

We have already seen *dao*, the Way, as a central term in both Confucianism and Daoism, where it means the ideal socio-ethical order and the natural order, respectively. More abstractly, we can view *dao* as simply order or pattern. We have also seen the Daoist claim (actually shared by Confucians but not given so much emphasis by them) that change is not a secondary characteristic of things but a fundamental reality. And finally, there is the concept of *qi*, or "psycho-physical stuff," the underlying and dynamic substance of which all existing things are composed. These three "unitary" concepts are the simplest building blocks of traditional Chinese cosmology.

Yin–yang

The simplest, most basic form of order is the division of unity into two, and the simplest pattern of change is bipolar alternation (day–night, open–closed, positive–negative). This is the essential insight of **yin–yang** theory, perhaps the most characteristic and pervasive concept in Chinese thought. The literal meanings of *yin* and *yang* are the shady and sunny sides of a hill, respectively, or simply darkness and light. A text from the mid-third century B.C.E. that became influential during the early Han describes this concept of cyclical alternation as the "round" or complete Way:

> Day and night make up a cycle; this is the Round Way. The threading of the moon through its twenty-eight lodges, so that Horn and Axletree are connected; this is the Round Way.[1] As the essences [of *yin* and *yang*] move through the four seasons, alternately upward and downward, they encounter each other; this is the Round Way. Something stirs and burgeons; burgeoning, it is born; born, it grows; growing, it matures; mature, it declines; declining, it dies; dead, it becomes latent [preceding another birth]; this is the Round Way.[2]

This describes *yin* and *yang* as a dynamic process, but the model also applies to static, complementary relationships. The following passage from the *Yijing*, or "Classic of Change," describes the relationship between the two six-line diagrams, or hexagrams, that represent pure *yang* and pure *yin*:

As Heaven is high and noble and Earth is low and humble,
so it is that **qian** [pure *yang*, Hexagram 1] and **kun** [pure
yin, Hexagram 2] are defined. The high and the low being
thereby set out, the exalted and the mean have their places
accordingly.[3]

The "exalted" and "mean" here refer to high and low social positions.
Thus the text is outlining a parallel relationship between the natural world and the social world, thereby legitimizing the social hierarchy
that had always characterized Chinese society.

Yin and *yang* are not substances or things but functional modes
of *qi*. *Yin* is *qi* in its dense, dark, sinking, receptive, "earthy" mode,
and *yang* denotes the light, bright, rising, creative, "heavenly" mode.
Thus *yin* and *yang* are the most fundamental pattern of change.
Although the meanings of *yin* and *yang* were originally gender-neu-
tral, in China's strongly patriarchal culture they were quickly associated
with female and male, respectively, and these in fact came to be among
the primary meanings of the terms in conventional usage. However,
these are secondary meanings based on assumptions about what constitute masculine and feminine characteristics. If one believes that
women are by nature more passive and "earthy" than men, then
one will associate *yin* with the female. But that particular assumption
can also be rejected without fundamentally altering the meanings and
usefulness of the *yin–yang* principle. It is true, though, that throughout the history of Chinese thought the gendered meanings of *yin*
and *yang* were seldom questioned.

Five Phases

The theory that the fluctuations of *qi* can be mapped not only according to a bipolar pattern but also according to a system of Five Phases
(**wuxing**) is usually attributed to the philosopher Zou Yan (c. 305–240
B.C.E.), whose school of thought was later called the *Yin–yang* School
(sometimes translated as the "Naturalist School"). The concept of the
Five Phases undoubtedly predated Zou Yan, but it was he who systematized the theory and first correlated it with the fluctuations of
human history. This theory became the basis of what is known as "correlative cosmology," which was extremely influential in nearly all
aspects of Chinese thought, especially the sciences.

The Five Phases are water, fire, wood, earth, and metal. *Wuxing* is often translated as "five elements," but that is misleading.

"Element" means a fundamental, indestructible, indivisible, unchanging substance, but this was never the understanding of the five *xing*. Rather, the Five Phases are (like *yin* and *yang*) phases in the ongoing transformative process of *qi*. Together the terms water, fire, wood, earth, and metal constitute a symbolic grammar of natural change and transformation, into which nearly every natural and human class of things can be categorized. For example, there are five colors, five tastes, five organs, five grains, five directions (including the center), and five visible planets (probably the origin of the system).

Five Phases theory involves two types of relations: the static correspondence or correlation of things in the same category, and the dynamic transformation of one category into another. For example, the five organs are spleen (wood), lungs (fire), heart (earth), liver (metal), and kidneys (water), while the five grains are wheat (wood), beans (fire), panicled millet (earth), hemp (metal), and millet (water). Since the spleen and wheat are both classified as "wood," a medical treatment of weakness in the spleen might involve eating wheat products (noodles). This would be an application of the static correspondence theory.

Early examples of the dynamic application of the theory included two sequences: the "conquest" sequence (probably the earliest) and the "production" sequence. One of the earliest applications of the theory was Zou Yan's idea that human history, in terms of the sequence of dynasties, follows these natural cycles. The conquest sequence is wood–metal–fire–water–earth: wood is "conquered" (chopped down) by metal; metal is melted by fire; fire is quenched by water; water is dammed by earth; and earth is contained within wood frames in the ancient "rammed earth" construction technique. The production sequence is wood–fire–earth–metal–water: wood when burnt makes fire; fire produces ashes; earth produces metal ores; metal when heated becomes liquid; and water makes vegetation grow.

The *Yin–yang* School is an early attempt to systematize a primordial Chinese insight: that the same abstract "natural law" governs both nature and culture, the empirical world and the spiritual world, the individual and the social. These concepts were incorporated into both Confucianism and Daoism during the Han dynasty.

Souls and Afterlife

Chinese views about souls and their fate after death are, in part, extensions of basic cosmological ideas. One of the earliest Chinese notions of life after death was the **Yellow Springs**, a vaguely defined, shadowy underworld. After the integration of Buddhist ideas into the Chinese popular worldview during the post-Han period of disunity, the idea of an underworld was elaborated into the picture of the Ten Kings of Hell, who judge the sins of the recently departed and either condemn them to punishment or promote them to heaven.

Conceptions of the individual soul and its fate after death were also elaborated and systematized in the Han dynasty, following the outline of the cosmological system. The basic idea is that there are two souls, corresponding to the *yin* and *yang* modes of *qi* that constitute the human being (remembering that *qi* includes matter, energy, and mind or spirit). The two souls are called the ***hun***, which is the *yang* soul, and the ***po***, the *yin* soul. The *hun* is the bright, airy, intelligent, "spiritual" aspect of the person, and the *po* is the dark, heavy, sensual, physical aspect. At death the *hun* and the *po* separate. The *hun* rises to Heaven and becomes a spirit (***shen***) or an ancestor (***zu***). The *po* stays with the physical body in the earth and becomes a ghost (***gui***). This, at least, is one of the simpler scenarios in a vast array of variations. In the ideal case—when the body has been properly buried with all the necessary rituals and the ancestral spirit is worshipped by surviving family members—the *hun* remains a contented member of the family and can even bestow benefits on it, while the *gui* stays with the body in the grave. But if those conditions are not met, the *gui* will become an unhappy or vengeful ghost who causes trouble for the family, and this is to be avoided at all cost.

The term for gods is the same as the term for spirits, *shen*, illustrating the close connection between gods and human beings. In fact, an ancestor can become a god, and some historical figures, such as Confucius, are honored with rituals indistinguishable from those performed for gods. Ancestor worship within individual families is also nearly indistinguishable from the worship of gods.

Non-dualism

The most significant aspect of these popular religious concepts is that Chinese conceptions of life and death, body and soul, humans and gods, are non-dualistic, based on the cosmology of *qi* and *yin–yang*. "Non-dualism," as it has come to be used in the study of East Asian religions, stakes out a middle ground between "monism" and "dualism."

Monism describes a system of thought in which only one thing is fundamentally real, and all observed distinctions are illusory. The best example of a monistic system of thought is the philosophy of Advaita Vedanta developed by the eighth-century C.E. Indian sage Shankara, based on the teachings of the *Upanishads*. In this system only *Brahman*—the unchanging, purely spiritual essence and power underlying all things—is real. All distinctions among things are *maya*, or illusion. A good example of the opposite, dualistic, position is the philosophy of the French thinker René Descartes (1596–1650), who said that there are two fundamentally real things: body (that which is extended in space) and mind (that which thinks). This philosophy influenced Western thinking into the twentieth century and beyond.

Non-dualism is emplified by *yin* and *yang*, which can be defined only in relation to each other. Differences are real, but they have a complementary or bipolar relation as aspects of a more fundamental order (the *dao*). North is not south, a positive electric charge is definitely different from a negative charge, but in both cases one term implies the other.

Differences are thus aspects of a more fundamental unity. By keeping this insight in mind we will be able to avoid such oversimplifications as saying that Chinese thinkers understand body and mind to be one, or that there is no difference between humans and gods.

Confucianism

The early Han emperors adopted a syncretic form of Daoism as a philosophy of government. But the sixth emperor, Wudi, who reigned from 140 to 87 B.C.E., dropped Daoism in favor of Confucianism. In this he was strongly influenced by the philosopher Dong Zhongshu (c. 179–104 B.C.E.), who developed a form of Confucianism that incorporated elements of *yin–yang* thought and correlative cosmology. Dong was especially concerned with developing a theory to explain and legitimate the authority of the emperor, basically by conflating the categories of rulership and sagehood.

But Dong's most significant contribution to the history of Chinese religion was his success in persuading Wudi to establish Confucianism as the official state ideology. This institutionalization took two forms. First, in 136 B.C.E. the government was reorganized under five ministries headed by "Scholars of the Five Classics." Then, in 124 B.C.E., an imperial college was established to train government officials in the Five Classics and their application to government, according to the principles of interpretation developed by Dong Zhong-shu and his colleagues. This was the first official canonization of a Chinese textual tradition.

Another Confucian text, the *Classic of Filiality* (**Xiaojing**), written anonymously in the Latter Han dynasty, has been extremely influential in Chinese society for almost 2000 years. Throughout East Asia "filial piety" is still more widely and strongly associated with Confucianism than any other virtue. Building on Confucius' statement that "filiality is the root of the Way" (*Analects* 1:2), the *Classic of Filiality* claims that the parent–child relationship reflects patterns in nature and in turn is the model for all social and political relations. Here again we see the social hierarchy grounded in and legitimized by Chinese cosmological theory.

One of the most interesting sections of the *Classic of Filiality* concerns the relationship between superiors and inferiors, beginning with parent and child. It is almost universally assumed today, even in China, that Confucianism teaches the necessity of absolute obedience to elders and superiors. But in fact Confucius himself had taught that a filial son should "gently remonstrate" with a parent who has done wrong (*Analects* 4:18). The *Classic of Filiality* devotes a whole section to the necessity to argue (**zheng**) with those above when the superior has lost sight of the Way:

> In ancient times, if the Son of Heaven had seven ministers to oppose [*zheng*] him, even if he had lost the Way he would not lose his empire ... If a father had even one son to remonstrate [*zheng*] with him, he still would not fall into evil ways. In the face of whatever is not right, the son cannot but remonstrate with his father, and the minister cannot but remonstrate with his prince. If it is not right, remonstrate! (section 15)[4]

"*Zheng*" is also the word used by Laozi to mean "struggle," which is to be avoided if one is to live a long life in harmony with the Way. This difference highlights the fact that the Confucian Dao is defined in moral terms, while the Daoist Dao is defined in terms of natural processes.

Confucianism for Women

Confucius taught only men, and literate men at that. Even today in mainland China it is rare for poor rural women to receive as much education as their brothers. But with the growing power of Confucianism in the Han, it is not surprising that women took an interest in it. In scholarly families it was not rare, even at that time, for women to learn to read—partly because it was largely their job to teach boys, in the home, until they started school at about the age of eight.

Patriarchal thinking was very deeply rooted in ancient China, and it was assumed that at least some of the virtues of women were different from those of men. Several women's versions of the classics were written, including the *Biographies of Virtuous Women* and *Admonitions for Women* in the Han, and the *Classic of Filiality for Women* in the Tang. The *Biographies of Virtuous Women*, by the (male) bibliographer Liu Xiang (79–78 B.C.E.), contains the story of Mencius' mother as a prominent example of a woman sage. She raised Mencius by herself, and was so concerned with his education that she moved three times seeking a better social environment for her son.[5] The way a woman becomes a Confucian sage is by fully realizing the womanly Way, and in ancient China that meant being a good wife and mother.

Admonitions for Women was written by Ban Zhao in the Latter Han. She was the sister of Ban Gu, the compiler of the official history of the Han dynasty, which she completed after his death. She was perhaps the earliest prominent female intellectual in China. Given her accomplishments, it may be surprising to find that much of her advice to young women encourages them to be lowly and humble, modest and yielding.[6] However, Ban Zhao was clearly a woman of her time and place, and in order to achieve what she did she had no choice but to accept the reigning worldview. But she does argue for the importance of educating girls and women, and in applying the *yin–yang* principle to the relationship between men and women, she stresses their mutuality and interdependence as much as the principle that *yin* is naturally subordinate to *yang*:

> The Way of husband and wife is intimately connected with yin and yang and relates the individual to gods and ancestors. Truly it confirms the great principle of Heaven and Earth.

> If a husband be unworthy, then he possesses nothing by which to control his wife. If a wife be unworthy, the she possesses nothing with which to serve her husband. ... As a

> matter of fact, in practice these two [the controlling of
> women by men and the serving of men by women] work out
> in the same way.[7]

Like the author of the *Classic of Filiality*, Ban Zhao here is tracing the correspondence of cosmological and ethical principles. Thus Han correlative cosmology became the systematic logic underlying Confucian ethics.

Post-Han Confucianism

After the Han, few original thinkers were attracted to Confucian thought until its revival in the late Tang and early Song. The tradition had been so closely associated with the Han dynasty that, when the dynasty fell, Confucianism was discredited. Confucian principles remained the official philosophy of government and education, and Confucian writers concentrated on writing commentaries to the classics. In the early Tang dynasty an officially sponsored edition of these was published: *Orthodox Interpretations of the Five Classics*, compiled by Kong Yingda (587–648), a descendant of Confucius. But none of these works developed Confucian thought in new ways until the Confucian renaissance in the Song.

Early signs of this renaissance appeared in the late Tang. Han Yu (768–824), one of the great writers in Chinese history, felt that Daoism and Buddhism had sapped Chinese civilization of its moral foundations. One of his most famous essays, a memorial to the Tang emperor, can only be described as a diatribe against Buddhism. In it he opposes a plan for the emperor officially to receive in the palace a relic of the Buddha from a delegation of Buddhist monks. Han Yu says that the Buddha did not understand proper social relations and would not have been taken seriously when alive. Moreover, he was a foreigner who dressed differently and did not speak Chinese. "How then, when he has long been dead, could his rotten bones, the foul and unlucky remains of this body, be rightly admitted to the palace?"[8]

Behind Han Yu's apparent xenophobia is the belief that neither Buddhism nor Daoism provided adequate moral and intellectual support for Chinese society and government. Han Yu therefore tried to revive the Way of the Sages. In his essay "Essentials of the Moral Way" (*Yuandao*) he argues that the Confucian Way of humanity and rightness (*ren* and *yi*), which had declined after Mencius, is better for

China than the Ways of Daoism and Buddhism. He even developed a new style of prose, which he called "the literature of antiquity" (*guwen*), which he felt was closer to the style of the ancient classics than the more elaborate and structured prose styles then in fashion. The *guwen* style later became the standard in the Song dynasty, when Han Yu's ideas finally took root.

Daoism

Historical Development

For the first sixty years or so of the Han dynasty, the most influential school of thought at the Han court was a syncretic form of Daoism known as **Huang-Lao,** named after the mythic Yellow Emperor (**Huangdi**) and Laozi. The *Huainanzi*, a text named for the King of Huainan, Liu An, who sponsored and edited the work, is a compendium of the teachings of this school. It incorporates Daoist cosmology and the theory of governing by *wuwei*, as found in the *Laozi*, with techniques of spiritual cultivation such as those found in *Zhuangzi* and another early syncretic text, the *Guanzi*.[9] Huang-Lao thought provides a theory and methods by which the ruler can become a sage by ruling in accordance with the Dao. The *Huainanzi* was presented in 139 B.C.E. by Liu An to his nephew the Han emperor Wudi, who at the time was being advised by Dong Zhongshu to reject Huang-Lao in favor of Confucianism. As we saw in the previous section, Wudi decided in favor of Dong, and the Huang-Lao school slipped into obscurity—but its ideas continued to shape Daoist political movements and thought.

In the Latter Han dynasty, especially during its decline in the second century C.E., there were several movements predicting that Laozi would return to reign over an era of "Great Peace" (*taiping*). Thus Laozi underwent a transformation from revered sage to deity, a divine representation of the cosmic Dao.[10] In this form he appeared in a series of revelations, starting in 142 C.E., to a man named Zhang Daoling, in what is today the province of Sichuan in southwest China. Laozi, in the form of **Taishang Laojun** (Lord Lao the Most High), dictated to Zhang Daoling a series of instructions on morality, meditation, the cure of disease through rituals of petition to various deities, ritual recitation of the *Laozi*, and social organization. Zhang Daoling became known as the first Celestial Master (Tianshi), a title that has been handed down to his male descendants to this day (the present Celestial Master lives in Taiwan) in a tradition known as the Way of the **Celestial Masters** (*Tianshidao*). On the basis of these instructions a Daoist community was formed that numbered, by the end of the Han dynasty, some 400,000 members. The texts, along with the *Laozi* and the *Zhuangzi*, became the core of the Daoist canon (**Daozang**), a collection that today includes 1426 titles.[11]

In 215, Zhang Daoling's grandson Zhang Lu, the third Celestial Master, entered into a treaty with the northern state of Wei, pledging loyalty and spiritual support to that state in exchange for protection. However, the Daoists were required to disperse throughout the kingdom, which weakened their social base. The Wei were conquered by the Western Jin in 266, and in 316 its capital, Chang'an, was conquered by the nomadic **Xiongnu**. Many of the Chinese aristocracy emigrated to the south, where they came into contact with new religious practices, including alchemy.

In about 320 a southerner named Ge Hong (283–343) wrote a book called *The Master Who Embraces Simplicity*, or **Baopuzi**, which reflects the incorporation of southern Chinese traditions of alchemy into Daoism. By undergoing a lengthy process of purification and self-cultivation, followers would be able to create an elixir that would transform them into immortals, or *xian*, occupying the Heaven of Great Purity (**Taiqing**), higher than the heaven occupied by the deified Laozi (**Taishang**, the Most High).

Between 364 and 370 another series of revelations came to a medium named Yang Xi, who worked for an old southern aristocratic family named Xu, near modern Nanjing. These new revelations came from various deities called "Perfected Ones" (*zhenren*, a term from *Zhuangzi*) in the Heaven of Highest Purity (**Shangqing**), which was claimed to be the highest of the three Daoist heavens. Many of the Shangqing texts were collected and edited by Tao Hongjing (456–536), an accomplished scholar and alchemist, who really completed the merging of the southern alchemical traditions with Celestial Master Daoism. The Shangqing tradition is called **Maoshan** Daoism, because both the Xu family and Tao Hongjing had retreats on Mt. Mao (Maoshan), near Nanjing.

The Shangqing texts include further instructions on the alchemical production of elixirs, and more advanced meditations and visualizations designed to enable the individual practitioner to purify his or her *qi* in order to become aware of the divinities that reside in the human body. They also include breathing techniques, fasting, and gymnastic exercises, for the spiritual exercises are rooted in the physical body. The Shangqing school emphasized individual spiritual practice and tended to appeal to the élite, many of whom were government officials. In this sense, then, they were Confucians in their public lives, while privately following Daoism.

In the 390s Ge Hong's grandnephew Ge Chaofu published a text that he claimed had originated with Ge Hong's great-uncle Ge Xuan. This became the kernel of a body of Daoist texts called the **Lingbao** (Numinous Jewel) scriptures. These writings reformulated much Shangqing and Buddhist material, using Han cosmology to organize and "Sinify" the Buddhist elements.[12] The Lingbao texts were the first to incorporate into Daoism confession, public rituals, moral precepts, and the Buddhist ideas of *karma* and rebirth. Lingbao public rituals became extremely popular among ordinary people in the Tang dynasty, and many are still performed today.

Since the fifth century the Celestial Masters, Shangqing, and Lingbao scriptures have been merged into the Daoist canon, the present version of which was compiled in 1445. Daoism thrived during the Tang dynasty, partly because the Tang ruling house believed themselves to be part of Laozi's clan and therefore generously supported and patronized institutional Daoism.

Daoist Beliefs and Practices

The core of Daoist religious practice is meditation and ritual. The aim of both is to enhance spiritual and physical health, with the ultimate aim (for very serious practitioners) of achieving an identity with the Dao that is tantamount to immortality. The symbols of this goal are the *xian* (immortal or transcendent) and the *zhenren* (perfected person). Daoist rituals are also practiced by and for entire communities, for their success and well-being. On the individual level, in addition to meditation, Daoist practices include dietary practices and, in former times, alchemy and certain sexual rituals.

The cosmology of the Daoist religion, like that of classical Daoism, is based on the concept of Dao as the natural, cosmic order. But the religious conception goes further: here the Dao acts consciously in human history by incarnating itself in different forms at key moments. Laozi, as we have seen, was an incarnation of the Dao. Other deities reside in the human body, which is an integral part of the Dao and a microcosm of the spiritual universe.

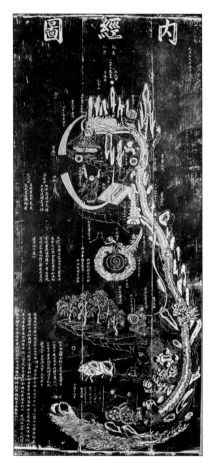

*A Daoist diagram of the human body and its internal deities: a microcosm of the spiritual universe. The deities are located in the head, heart, and abdomen, which are the body's three "cinnabar fields" (*dantian*).*

The three highest deities are called the Three Pure Ones (**Sanqing**), who correspond to the three sets of revelations mentioned above, although they are not the sources of the revelations. They each preside over one of the three Daoist heavens, which are arrayed hierarchically above the six heavens populated by all the other Chinese deities. Table 1 summarizes these relationships, with the highest at the top.

Daoist physiology involves another three-fold set of terms. Here the three fundamental substances, or forms of *qi*, that are manipulated and cultivated in Daoist religious practice correspond with the three centers of spiritual energy in the human body, which are called "cinnabar fields" (***dantian***) and are located in the head, chest, and abdomen (see Table 2). Furthermore, each cinnabar field is the residence of a deity who simultaneously resides in the stars. These three are called the "Three Ones" (**Sanyi**); by visualizing them the adept forges a spiritual connection with the astral/celestial world:

> The meditation practice that went with this [set of beliefs] was mainly a technique of visualization—of the different colors associated with the organs to strengthen their *qi*, of

TABLE 1: DAOIST COSMOLOGY AND REVELATIONS			
Heavens	**Pure Ones**	**Texts**	**Main Sources**
Shangqing (Highest Purity)	Yuanshi Tiancun (Heavenly Worthy of the Primordial Beginning)	Shangqing scriptures	Revelations to Yang Xi (364–370), edited by Tao Hongjing (456–536)
Taiqing (Great Purity)	Lingbao Tiancun (Heavenly Worthy of the Numinous Jewel)	Lingbao scriptures	Ge Chaofu (400) and others
Taishang (Most High)	Daode Tiancun (Heavenly Worthy of the Way and its Power)	Tianshi (Celestial Master) scriptures	Revelations to Zhang Daoling (142)

TABLE 2: DAOIST PHYSIOLOGY	
Substances	**Cinnabar fields (*dantian*)**
Shen, or "spirit," exemplified by the *hun* and *po* (*yang* and *yin* souls), which in Daoism number three and seven, respectively.	Head
Qi, or "vital breath," which can be manipulated in the body by the control of breathing, but is not the same as the air that is breathed.	Heart (or solar plexus)
Jing, or "vital essence," a condensed, visible form of *qi* that is best exemplified by semen and female sexual fluid.	Abdomen (below navel)

> the inner passways and palaces to learn the cosmic
> geography, of gods and immortals residing there to acquire
> familiarity with the divine figures, and of the planets and
> stars to merge with their power.[13]

Western students meeting Daoist religious beliefs and practices such as these often find them very remote from the Daoism they thought they knew in *Laozi* and *Zhuangzi*. Indeed, these aspects of Daoism do have independent sources in later revelations, as we have seen. But we should remember that the first of these revelations, those of the Celestial Masters, came from a divinized Laozi, and later Daoists continued to worship Laozi. Clearly they saw a connection between the text attributed to Laozi and the religion they actually practiced.

One important connection between the two phases of the tradition is that both imply that human beings are fully "at home" in the natural world—including their own bodies—although they can be alienated from it. By contemplating the natural/cosmic Dao both internally and externally, and by purifying oneself to facilitate that contemplation, one can make physically and spiritually real one's fundamental nature as an organic part of the Dao. Compared with most Western forms of spirituality, this is an extremely wholehearted acceptance of and focus on the physical body. In Daoism the body is essential to spiritual fulfillment.

The importance of the body in Daoism accounts for the significance of alchemy as a form of self-cultivation. Such Daoist masters as Ge Hong and Tao Hongjing developed the art and craft of synthesizing chemical substances that would, they believed, transform and purify their physiological substances into immortal forms. The most potent of these elixirs (**dan**) was cinnabar, a naturally occurring mineral with a deep, bright, red or vermilion color. This is a highly *yang* color (like blood and fire), which accounts for its potency. When heated, cinnabar transforms into mercuric sulfide, which is toxic, although it can be tolerated in small doses. There are a few recorded cases of alchemists deliberately overdosing on cinnabar, in the belief that what would appear to be their resulting deaths would actually be "deliverance from the corpse" or ascension to heaven.

Because of these potentially fatal consequences, the ingestion of elixirs was gradually replaced during the Tang dynasty by forms of Daoist meditation that use the language of laboratory substances and processes in reference to the internal substances of the body. This came to be known as "internal alchemy" (***neidan***, sometimes called "physiological alchemy" today), as opposed to the "external alchemy" (***waidan***) of the laboratory.

Daoist Women

There are elements of what we might anachronistically call "feminist" thought in the *Laozi*, such as the idea that aggression is counter-productive, the theme of fertility, the virtue of softness and yielding, and the image of the Dao as mother. But despite this emphasis on the feminine, it would be incorrect to assume that the author(s) of the *Laozi* conceived of the ideal sage–ruler as anything but a man. After the official recognition of Confucianism under Han Wudi, though, Confucianism became wedded to the prevailing patriarchal social system; Daoism and, eventually, Buddhism, became alternatives to that system. Daoism therefore attracted women in large numbers, and in the early Celestial Master communities women could be "**libationers**," the chief priests of local "parishes." This went far beyond any official possibilities for women in government.

Throughout the early imperial period there were many eminent female Daoist masters (***daoshi***). One of these was Bian Dongxuan in the seventh century, whose spiritual biography (or hagiography) describes her ascension to Heaven in broad daylight:

> On the fifteenth day of the seventh month from the hours of 7 to 9 a.m., heavenly music filled the void. Dense and impenetrable purple clouds wound around the storied buildings of the belvedere [convent]. The masses of the people saw Dongxuan ascend, with heavenly music preceding and following her, with standards and pennants spread out and arrayed. She departed straight to the south.[14]

Bian's biographer, Du Guangting (850–933), one of the foremost Daoist masters of his era, said that men and women can both achieve immortality, but their means of doing so are different and the titles they receive in heaven are different. This accords with the principle of *yin–yang*. But despite the differences, the women Du describes in his collection of biographies of female Daoist masters do the same kinds of things as their male counterparts. So the differences appear to be implicit assumptions rather than empirical observations.

Buddhism

Origins and Basic Doctrines

Buddhism arose in the fifth century B.C.E. in what today is Nepal, in the northeast of the Indian subcontinent. At that time the dominant religious tradition was Brahmanism, the ancient form of what is today called Hinduism. The Brahmans were priests who were empowered to perform the rituals to the gods of the *Vedas*, the ancient collections of hymns to the gods. Another class of religious specialists was the *sramanas*, or wandering ascetics, who practiced meditation and various austerities, such as fasting, trying to achieve spiritual purification.[15]

Three concepts in the Brahmanical worldview became important elements in Buddhist thought: *karma*, *samsara*, and *moksa*. The word *karma* literally means "action" or "deed," but the doctrine of *karma* is more complicated. It means that every intentional action or deed has a natural effect that will be experienced by the doer of the deed at some later point, and that the effect is determined by the moral character of the deed. Conversely, things that happen to a person are, in part, the natural effect of deeds he or she has done in the past. It is thus a doctrine of "moral causality."

Samsara means "cycle," and refers to the cycle of birth, death, and rebirth. In Brahmanism, every person has an immortal soul, which after death is reborn into a new body. The new person that we become is conditioned by our unresolved *karma*. That is, the effects of one's intentional deeds are not necessarily experienced during one lifetime, but they will be experienced. These two doctrines together describe a theory of justice. People may not experience the consequences of their actions during that same lifetime, but they will do so eventually. Unlike in the biblical religions, however, where there is a judge, these are natural effects. *Karma* is a natural law of moral cause and effect.

Although immortality has its attractions, living eternally also means dying eternally. Our souls may be immortal and inviolate, but to undergo the suffering of aging, disease, and death for eternity is not an attractive option. Moreover, rebirth as a human is extremely rare. In Buddhism there are six levels of *samsara* on which one can be reborn, depending on one's *karma*: gods, demigods, humans, animals, hungry ghosts, and demons. Hence the desirability of **moksa**, or "liberation" from the cycle of *samsara*. In Buddhism this is called **nirvana**, which literally means "extinguishing" or "snuffing out." If we think of *karma* as the energy that drives the wheel of *samsara*, then to achieve *nirvana* is to extinguish that energy, with the result that one is no longer reborn.

The man we know as "the Buddha," or Enlightened/Awakened One, was born the son of a king who wished to shelter him from the suffering of the world outside the palace grounds. His name was Siddhartha Gautama, of the Sakya clan. According to the stories that have been passed down (none of these details is historically verifiable), he was married and had a young son when he became curious about the world outside. With the help of a servant he sneaked out at night four times, each time seeing something he had never seen before. The first sight was a very old person, the second a diseased person, the third a corpse. These discoveries of human suffering and mortality made him realize for the first time his own fate. Then, on the fourth night, he saw a wandering holy person, or *sramana*, who seemed to have transcended suffering, and he vowed to follow that path. He left his family and luxurious lifestyle to become a wandering ascetic.

He practiced extreme austerities for several years, but these brought him no solution to the problem of suffering, and also made him so weak that he couldn't practice any more. So he decided to give up that path and follow a compromise between his early life of indulgence and the life of extreme self-denial. He called this the Middle Path.

Once he had regained his strength, he vowed to sit under a tree and meditate until he had discovered the cause and solution to suffering. In one climactic night, he purified his mind to the highest degree and experienced **bodhi**, or enlightenment (literally "awakening"). What he awakened to was the truths of the cause and solution to suffering, and these became the core of his teaching. From this point on he was known as the Buddha, and also as Sakyamuni (Sage of the Sakyas), or Sakyamuni Buddha. The complete enlightenment he experienced at this point is also referred to as *nirvana*, but should not be confused with the complete *nirvana* (**parinirvana**) that he experienced when he died at the age of eighty. The difference between the two stages of *nirvana* is that with the former Sakyamuni had neutralized all his previous *karma*, so that at the latter (*parinirvana*) he simply went out of existence, to be no longer reborn.

The Buddha taught for forty-five years, attracting a large number of disciples, whom he encouraged to spread his teachings (Buddhism is therefore the first missionary religion). The community of disciples was known as the Sangha. During the rainy season they would "retreat" to forest hermitages to practice meditation, and eventually this practice led to permanent monastic establishments. Although at first the Buddha wanted the Sangha to include only men, he was persuaded by his aunt (according to the tradition) to include women. The core of the Sangha comprised those who had taken certain vows of renunciation, but there were also lay members. Thus it came to be known as the "four-fold Sangha," including monks, nuns, laymen, and laywomen. Laypeople took five vows: (i) to abstain from taking life; (ii) to abstain from taking what is not given; (iii) to abstain from sexual misconduct; (iv) to abstain from false speech; (v) to abstain from intoxicants causing heedlessness.

Monks and nuns took five additional vows: (vi) to abstain from untimely eating; (vii) to abstain from dancing, singing, music, and unseemly shows; (viii) to abstain from wearing garlands, smartening with scents, and beautifying with perfumes; (ix) to abstain from the use of high and luxurious couches; (x) to abstain from accepting gold and silver (money).

A further large body of rules evolved for the monastic community, with more for nuns than monks. Nuns were to be considered junior to monks, even if they had been members far longer. The patriarchal social system of ancient India was thus imprinted on early Buddhism, even though there was no justification in Buddhist doctrine for discriminating against women.

The Buddha's teachings are called the **Dharma**, which means "law" or "truth." Among the earliest of these were the "Four Noble Truths," which may be considered the core of Buddhist doctrine. First, life necessarily involves *dukkha*, or "suffering." This term really means "unsatisfactoriness": the anxiety and frustration that humans inevitably experience. It does not mean that every moment of life is necessarily unsatisfactory, but that in some way, even indirectly, all ordinary experiences somehow entail frustration or suffering. For example, even when we experience pleasure, on some level we know that all pleasures are impermanent. Second, the cause of suffering is desire, or craving. We crave things—including life itself—only to find that they are impermanent. Third, to eliminate suffering we must eliminate craving. Fourth, the way to eliminate craving is the "Eightfold

Path": (i) right views (understanding the worldview taught by the Buddha); (ii) right intention (deciding to follow the path); (iii) right speech (being truthful); (iv) right action (doing no harm to other living beings); (v) right livelihood (making one's living without causing harm to any living beings); (vi) right effort (making the effort to purify one's mind of craving); (vii) right mindfulness (being aware of the causes of one's thoughts, intentions, and desires); (viii) right concentration (practicing meditation in order to purify the mind). The elements of the Eightfold Path are also referred to in three groups: Wisdom (i–ii), Morality (iii–v), and Concentration or Meditation (vi–viii).

Besides the Four Noble Truths, one of the first teachings, and the most important for a philosophical understanding of Buddhism, was the doctrine of "no-self," or *anatman*. This was a direct repudiation of one of the central beliefs in the philosophy that was then evolving in the Brahmanical tradition. In sacred texts called the *Upanishads*, which had begun to be compiled around the eighth century B.C.E., the philosophical underpinnings of the gods and rituals of the *Vedas* are developed. The two central terms there are *brahman*—the ultimate, spiritual ground of all existing things—and *atman*—the immortal soul, the ultimate selfhood, of every human being. After death the *atman* is reborn, or transmigrates, into a new body. The basic message of the *Upanishads* is that *brahman* and *atman* are essentially the same; that the individual human soul is the same as the "world soul"; it is immortal, unchanging, and absolute.

The Buddha's doctrine of *anatman* literally means "no *atman*": there is no immortal, unchanging self or soul. Buddhism takes as a premise that all things are impermanent, or constantly changing: what a thing is at one moment does not exist in the next moment. Thus all that exists are momentary states, called *dharmas*, or elements of existence (using the word in a different sense from "Dharma" as the teachings).

According to this doctrine, a person is a temporary collection of constantly changing *dharmas*. An early Buddhist analysis claims that there are five of these that constitute a person; they are called the Five Skandhas, or Aggregates: Form (body), Sensation (sense organs), Perception (mental registering of sensory input), Will or karmic predisposition (the predisposition to act in certain ways due to our unresolved *karma*), and Consciousness (awareness). None of these is what we identify as our "self." What we normally think of as the self is some permanent center linking these five elements, but the Buddha's point is that every human experience can be described and explained completely in terms of the Five Skandhas. Thus there is neither evidence nor need for an underlying "self" to account fully for human experience.

The real point of the doctrine of no-self is soteriological (having to do with "salvation," or in the Buddhist context, liberation from the cycle of rebirth). It is the mistaken notion of a "self" that lies at the root of our tendency to crave and dislike things or other people, whom I perceive as different from me. But in fact, each of us is a temporary local system in the cosmic flow of events—just as a hurricane is a temporary, constantly changing, arbitrarily defined subsystem of the global weather system.

All of these intellectual mistakes and their emotional effects are based on the erroneous habit of seeing processes as things, or unchanging essences. The Buddhist doctrine of no-self—and its later elaboration in the theory of emptiness—is really an attack on the universal human tendency to see the world as a collection of discrete, essentially unchanging things. The Buddhist worldview, with impermanence as its fundamental premise, sees the world as a network of causes and effects in which all "things" are interdependent. This is the early Buddhist doctrine of "dependent origination," which states that everything is dependent on everything else for its very existence and nature.

The Buddha, the Dharma, and the Sangha came to be known as the "**Three Jewels**" or Treasures of Buddhism, the three fundamental pillars of the tradition. To become a Buddhist requires one to take the "Triple Refuge": "I take refuge in the Buddha, I take refuge in the Dharma, I take refuge in the Sangha." This is the fundamental Buddhist declaration of faith in the Buddha as a human being who has transcended suffering and rebirth, in the efficacy of his teachings to enable others to do the same, and in the Sangha as a community that is conducive to achieving that goal.

In early Buddhism and in one major branch today, the Buddha is regarded simply as a human being, not a deity. And although the Triple Refuge is an initial statement of faith, one of the Buddha's teachings was that followers should not accept their truth on his word alone, but should try them out for themselves and see if they have the predicted effect of reducing suffering. Thus Buddhist teaching is pragmatic: it is true if it works. The point of the teaching is not just to understand, but to put the doctrines into practice.

Early Chinese Buddhism

Ancient China was connected to ancient India by branches of the Silk Road, a vast network of trade routes centered in Central Asia. The main route connecting the two regions was a treacherous path, reaching altitudes of about 19,000 feet, through the Hindu Kush from modern Pakistan to Afghanistan. It was along this route that Buddhism spread from northern India into Central Asia, and from there along the main east–west routes into China. The first mention of Buddhism in Chinese sources dates from the first century C.E., about 400 years after the death of the Buddha. Buddhist monks from India traveled with merchants to offer spiritual protection on their difficult journeys and to spread the Dharma. They established monasteries along the way that functioned as inns for merchant travelers.

At this time Buddhism was in the process of splitting into two main branches. The newer branch called itself the **Mahayana**, which means "Larger (or Greater) Vehicle," and this branch called those who kept to the older ways the **Hinayana**, or "Smaller (Lesser) Vehicle." The "vehicle" is the means to salvation, or *nirvana*. Mahayana was called the larger vehicle because it claimed to accommodate more people: one did not have to be a monk or a nun to have a reasonable expectation of achieving *nirvana* in this life, as one did in the older tradition. (Members of the older tradition did not themselves refer to it as Hinayana, because that was a pejorative term.) One of the schools of this older tradition was called **Theravada**, which means the "Teachings of the Elders," suggesting that this was closer to the original form of Buddhism. This is the only "Hinayana" school that still survives, so it has become customary to refer to these two branches as Mahayana and Theravada. Theravada today is found mainly in South and Southeast Asia (Sri Lanka, Burma, Cambodia, Thailand). Mahayana is the branch that predominates today in East Asia (China, Japan, Korea).

A third branch of Buddhism is called **Vajrayana**, which means "Diamond Vehicle." The diamond is a metaphor for the enlightened mind. This branch evolved in Tibet, to which Buddhism spread in the seventh century, but is also found today in Mongolia (whose leaders, or Khans, adopted it in the sixteenth century), and there is one school of Vajrayana (Shingon) in Japan.

Mahayana Buddhism differed from Theravada in a number of important respects. First, it was based on new scriptures, mostly written in Sanskrit, with some later texts written in Chinese. Popular new Mahayana *sutras* (texts claiming to be the words of the Buddha) included: the *Lotus Sutra*; the *Prajña-paramita* (Perfection of Wisdom) *sutras*, including the **Heart Sutra** and the **Diamond Sutra**; the *Pure Land sutras*, which gave rise to a whole new school of Buddhism; and the **Platform Sutra**, written in Chinese and central to the new Chan (Zen) school.

Second, the chief model for enlightenment in Mahayana is the bodhisattva, whereas in Theravada it is Sakyamuni Buddha, a historical person. The original meaning of *bodhisattva* ("enlightened being") was a Buddha-to-be: for example, Sakyamuni in his previous lives. In Mahayana the bodhisattva became a being who has achieved enlightenment, but who vows to remain in *samsara* until all other sentient beings are enlightened. Thus the bodhisattva is characterized chiefly by wisdom and compassion. The full "Bodhisattva Vow" is as follows:

> However innumerable the sentient beings, I vow to save them all.
> However inexhaustible the passions [e.g. desires], I vow to extinguish them all.
> However immeasurable the *dharmas*, I vow to master them all.
> However incomparable the truth of the Buddha, I vow to attain it.

Third, Mahayana Buddhism, unlike Theravada, can be regarded as a theistic tradition. While Theravada accepts the existence of gods, it believes they are irrelevant to the Buddhist path; they can be of assistance for worldly goals, but they cannot help one achieve enlightenment, because they have not achieved it themselves—they are still in *samsara*. The Buddha himself was a human being, not a god. But as Buddhism spread through northern India and Central Asia it assimilated local gods, redefining them as Buddhas and Bodhisattvas. Thus Mahayana Buddhism acquired a theistic dimension, with Buddhas (now multiple) and Bodhisattvas as the chief objects of worship. Some of the most popular are:

Buddhas: Sakyamuni (**Shijiamouni** in Chinese, or Shijia for short), the historical Buddha.
Amitabha (**Amituo**), the Buddha of Infinite Light, who presides over the Pure Land (see below).
Vairocana (**Loshana**), the cosmic Buddha.

Bodhisattvas: Manjusri (**Wenshu**), the Bodhisattva of Wisdom.
Avalokitesvara (Guanyin), the Bodhisattva of Compassion. This bodhisattva was originally portrayed as a male, but became female in China. She was and is especially popular among women.
Maitreya (**Mile**), the Buddha of the Future.

A fourth difference between the two branches is that Mahayana offers laypeople new roles and possibilities for salvation. In Theravada, lay Buddhists are considered to be following the Eightfold Path, but they are not as far along the path as monks and nuns. In Mahayana, however, the possibility of enlightenment in this life is explicitly granted to laypeople. This is based, in part, on the new philosophical principle of the "universal Buddha-nature."

Mahayana Buddhism also developed distinctly new philosophical positions. The most important is the concept of **emptiness** (*kong*) which is actually an expansion of the concept of no-self, using exactly the same logic but applying it to all things, rather than just people. The basic concept is that, because all things are interdependent and impermanent, they lack independent, autonomous natures. Thus "emptiness" really means "emptiness of self-nature." Or since emptiness means the lack of independence, to state it positively we can say that emptiness means interdependence. As one of the greatest Mahayana thinkers, the Indian philosopher **Nagarjuna** (second century C.E.), put it, "Emptiness is dependent origination."[16]

Another central Mahayana doctrine is the concept of universal Buddha-nature. This means that all sentient beings (and, according to later Mahayana thinkers, even inanimate objects) are manifestations of Buddhahood. Another way of putting this is to say that all beings have "inherent enlightenment." If all things are interdependent, and their interdependence (or emptiness) is their fundamental nature, then all things share the same nature as buddhas and bodhisattvas.

This reasoning has the further implication that *nirvana* and *samsara* must be interdependent, which is to say that they share the same nature (emptiness), and are therefore not fundamentally distinct. Again, Nagarjuna put this boldly by saying that there is no difference between *nirvana* and *samsara*. This appears to be a paradoxical statement, because in their original formulations, *nirvana* was defined as the negation of *samsara*; *nirvana* is achieved when one leaves

Seated Buddha (about 45 feet tall) and a standing bodhisattva at Yungang, near Datong, from the Northern Wei period (c. 490). The Northern Wei dynasty adopted Buddhism and sponsored much monumental sculpture.

or transcends the *samsaric* cycle. However, following Nagarjuna, we can say that *nirvana* is the true nature of *samsara*; the ultimate truth is found in, and only in, the mundane world of ordinary experience.

Let us take a step back now and reflect on some of the larger patterns in Chinese religious thought. One generalization we might make about Confucianism and Daoism is that they both, in different ways, strongly affirm the ultimate meaning and value of this world and ordinary life. Confucianism focuses on the social world, starting with the family, as the place where ultimate values are learned and put into practice. Although there is a connection with a transcendent reality (Heaven), religious knowledge is not obtained through revelation; it is obtained through learning the ways of the sages, who were just human beings, and (in the Mencian tradition) through self-knowledge. Similarly, in classical Daoism, the "constant Way" is the ordering principle of the natural world, and in the Daoist religion the human body is the raw material for the creation of gods. Laozi too said, "The world is a sacred vessel" (*Laozi* 29).

Buddhism, when it entered China, was perceived to be rather world-denying. Not only did it appear (at least on the surface) to teach that this world is full of suffering and needs to be transcended, but it also encouraged people to leave their families and live in secluded monastic settings, seeking individual liberation from both the natural and the social worlds. But some elements in the Buddhist tradition were more consonant with Chinese world-affirmation. Nagarjuna's philosophy, for example, clearly offered ways of seeing ultimate value in the natural and social worlds. It was these elements that the Chinese focused on, and developed even further in the new schools of Buddhism that arose in China.

New Buddhist Schools in China

The Mahayana Buddhism that spread into China starting from the first century took several centuries to become fully digested by the Chinese. Early Mahayana texts were written in Sanskrit, which of course had to be translated into Chinese. Central Asian Buddhists were key figures in this laborious process, notably the great Kumarajiva (350–413), who led a team of translators in Chang'an. Several Chinese Buddhist pilgrims made epic journeys to India to bring back scriptures to be translated, including Faxian (fourth–fifth century) and Xuanzang (seventh century). But until about the fourth century, Buddhism was largely the religion of foreign monks residing in China. It was at first regarded by the Chinese as being similar to Daoism, because both had professional priesthoods and both seemed (at least to Confucians) to be oriented toward individual spiritual transformation rather than the transformation of society.

All of the traditions of Indian Mahayana Buddhism were represented in China, but here we will focus on the new Chinese schools: **Pure Land**, **Tiantai**, **Huayan**, and **Chan**. These all had roots in the Indian tradition, but they were sufficiently new to warrant consideration as Chinese creations. All of them reflected Chinese religious sensibilities and needs.

PURE LAND Pure Land (*Jingtu*) Buddhism is based on three sutras, originally written in Sanskrit, which focus on the Buddha Amitabha (Amituo in Chinese) and the vows he made while still a bodhisattva. His central vow was that, if he were to achieve the complete enlightenment of a Buddha, he would preside over a heavenly paradise, called Sukhavati (Pure or Happy Land), into which he would cause anyone who faithfully called on his name to be reborn. This would not be *nirvana*, but it would be a long lifetime with no suffering, spent in the company of Amitabha and many bodhisattvas. From there the person would be reborn one final time as a human and instantly achieve Buddhahood. The penultimate life in the Pure Land would therefore be a reward for faith in the compassion and salvific power of Amitabha, and would be the last step before *nirvana*.

One of the premises of Pure Land Buddhism was that the present age—the period of disunity between the Han and Sui-Tang—was in decline. Like the theory of rebirth on the individual level, Buddhism has a theory of cosmic cycles. Sakyamuni is the Buddha of the present cycle, but this cosmos will come to an end and a new one will appear, presided over by a new Buddha (Maitreya, the Buddha of the Future). The present cycle will go through three periods: (i) the period of the Correct Dharma (*zhengfa*), during which people can hear and understand the Buddha's teachings directly; (ii) the period of the Pseudo Dharma (*xiangfa*), during which a semblance of the true teachings will be taught, and only the most capable will understand it; and (iii) the period of the End of the Dharma (*mofa*), when people will no longer be capable of achieving enlightenment at all. Believing that they were living in this final age, Pure Land teachers felt that people of their day required the compassion and "grace" of Amitabha Buddha in order to transcend *samsara* via the Pure Land.

The appeal of Pure Land Buddhism to ordinary people was far greater than that of other schools, in which the monastic lifestyle was central although not required. The basic practice in Pure Land is not meditation but chanting the name of Amitabha Buddha. In Chinese, the chant is simply, *Nanwu Amituofo* ("Homage to Amitabha Buddha"). This can be done silently or out loud, individually or in groups, without any alteration of one's ordinary lifestyle.

In China, Pure Land Buddhism never developed into an institutionally distinct sect, as it did in Japan (where it is by far the most popular form of Buddhism). But the Pure Land practice of chanting the Buddha's name (*nianfo*) became very popular among common people in China, and was also incorporated into the practice regimens of the monastic schools. Thus it became part of what it meant to be a Buddhist in medieval China.

TIANTAI AND HUAYAN Tiantai is the name of a mountain (Heavenly Terrace) southeast of Hangzhou on the east coast, where the temple of the school's founder, Zhiyi (538–597) is located. By the sixth century, so many different Buddhist texts and traditions had been imported from India that some Chinese practitioners found it difficult to determine which were earlier and which later, which presupposed others, and how to make sense of apparent contradictions. Zhiyi made sense of the variety of Buddhist teachings in three ways: by focusing primarily on a single text, the *Lotus Sutra*; by devising a classification system of the Buddha's teachings, in which the *Lotus* is described as his last, most advanced doctrine; and by developing a systematic philosophy based on a synthesis of the teachings and practices of other schools.

The culmination of this synthetic philosophy is the notion of the "true suchness" (*zhenru*) of things. This is understood as the "mean" between the fundamental emptiness of things and their "provisional existence." That is, emptiness does not mean non-existence. Things do have a kind of existence; it is just that they lack self-existence, or self-nature. "Suchness" expresses this middle ground in a positive manner, rather than the negative formulation of "emptiness." It is therefore an attempt to clarify the notion of emptiness, and it also satisfies the more affirmative, world-accepting sensibility of the Chinese.

The Huayan or "Flower Garland" school of Chinese Buddhism takes its name from the sutra that it regards as the Buddha's final, highest teaching: the **Avatamsaka** (Flower Garland, or *Huayan* in Chinese) **Sutra**. This very long sutra develops the concept of the interpenetration of all things (or *dharmas*), based on the concept of emptiness. Since all things are fundamentally interdependent, and therefore each individual thing fully manifests the principle of emptiness, it can be concluded that each individual thing, down to the tiniest grain of sand, fully contains the ultimate truth of every other thing. This "all in one, one in all" doctrine is a more world-affirming formulation than the easily misunderstood concept of emptiness, which risks being interpreted as a form of nihilism.

CHAN The most successful school of Chinese Buddhism was the Chan or "Meditation" school. The word Chan comes from a Chinese transliteration (**channa**) of the Sanskrit word *dhyana*, which means a state of meditative concentration, or just meditation. When it was brought to Japan in the late twelfth century, the Chinese character for Chan was pronounced Zen.[17]

The Chan school traces its lineage back to a story about the Buddha and one of his disciples, Kasyapa. Once, when the Buddha was about to preach and his disciples were gathered around him, he merely held up a flower, saying nothing. All the disciples looked puzzled except Kasyapa, who smiled with understanding. The Buddha handed him the flower and said that he was passing down to Kasyapa a teaching beyond words. Chan describes itself as a "mind-to-mind transmission" that cannot be captured by words, and regards Kasyapa as its first patriarch. This notion is also expressed by a poem that is attributed to its twenty-eighth Indian patriarch, Bodhidharma, who is said to have brought the teaching from India to China in 520, and so is also known as the first Chinese patriarch:

> A special transmission outside the teaching,
> Not based on the written word;
> Directly pointing to the human mind,
> Achieving Buddhahood by seeing one's nature.

The second couplet states that the aim of Chan practice is self-knowledge, and that the "self" thus known is one's inherent enlightenment, or Buddha-nature. The first couplet is often misunderstood to mean that Chan is opposed to scriptural study. The key word in the first couplet, though, is "transmission" (**chuan**), which refers not to the tradition as a whole but to the process by which the tradition is handed down from master to disciple. The enlightenment experience is such that it cannot be achieved solely by studying texts because it is an intuitive experience, not an intellectual one. But this does not mean that scriptural study is not important, as the actual practice of Chan Buddhists demonstrates.

Very little is known of the historical Bodhidharma—there are a couple of short texts that he may have written—but myths abound. It is said that he crossed the Yangzi River on a single reed; that he settled at Shaolin Monastery (legendary home of the Chinese martial arts); that he was so determined to achieve enlightenment that he sat in meditation facing a wall for nine years until his legs atrophied and fell off; that he cut off his eyelids so that he would not fall asleep; and that when his eyelids fell to the ground they sprouted into tea plants, thus introducing tea to China. (Tea, originally grown in India, was in fact popularized by Buddhist monks who used it to help them stay awake during long periods of meditation.)

Chan monks in meditation at Fayuan Temple in Beijing. Fayuan Temple, originally built in 696, is today the headquarters of the Chinese Buddhist Association and is home to the Beijing Buddhist Academy, a kind of Buddhist university.

Bodhidharma (Damo in Chinese) is a Chan icon, depicted in thousands of ink paintings by Chinese, Japanese, and Korean Zen masters and artists, because he symbolizes a fierce determination to achieve enlightenment by sitting in meditation (**zuochan**, or *zazen* in Japanese). But how could Chan lay special claim to meditation, which had been part of the Buddhist tradition since the very beginning? The answer is that Chan was in part a reaction against what some perceived to be the excessive interest in philosophy of the Tiantai and Huayan schools. While neither of them ignored meditation, their focus on individual scriptures (the *Lotus* and *Avatamsaka Sutras*) and their highly developed and sophisticated philosophical systems laid them open to the criticism that they had lost sight of the original purpose of the Buddha's teaching, which was to reduce suffering.

The next hero in the Chan "creation myth" is the Sixth Patriarch, **Huineng** (638–713). His story is told in one of the central texts of Chan, the *Platform Sutra of the Sixth Patriarch*, the only Buddhist sutra that does not claim to be the words of the Buddha. Huineng is depicted here as an illiterate young man who comes to hear the Dharma from the Fifth Patriarch, Hongren, but is merely given a job working in the monastery kitchen. When Hongren decides to retire and must choose a successor, he challenges all the monks to write verses demonstrating their levels of enlightenment. Everyone expects the winner to be Shenxiu, the senior monk. Shenxiu writes a verse on the wall, which Hongren praises, although he is secretly disappointed. Huineng, the illiterate kitchen helper, composes his own verse, which someone writes on the wall for him. Hongren recognizes genuine enlightenment in this verse, and names Huineng as his successor. Instead of taking over the monastery, though, Huineng flees to the south because he is regarded as something of a usurper.

Modern-day scholars have shown this story to be a complete fiction, but it is important for what Huineng represents: the possibility of enlightenment by an ordinary person, even one who is illiterate. Here again we see a uniquely Chinese expression of the Mahayana doctrine of inherent enlightenment and universal Buddha-nature.

The history of Chan during the late Tang is very hazy. As far as we can tell, in the Tang there was "an elaborate network of masters, each transmitting his own creative understanding of Buddhism to numerous followers who wandered from master to master," mostly in southern China.[18] This network was later (during the Song) systematized into five lineages or "houses." Of these, the two major ones were the Linji and Caodong lineages.

The **Linji** line (Rinzai in Japanese) is named for Linji Yixuan (d. 866), who was a very colorful personality known for shocking his students out of their habitual ways of thinking by shouting at them and hitting them, or by redirecting their attention away from theory to the simple need to practice awareness of the present moment. The **Caodong** line (Soto in Japanese) is named for Caoshan Benji (840–901) and his teacher Dongxuan Liangjie (807–869), whose teaching methods were less provocative.

These lineages go back to Mazu Daoyi (709–788) and Shitou Xiqian (700–790), the two most influential teachers of their time. Mazu, the progenitor of the Linji lineage, also occasionally used kicks and blows in his teaching. It was mainly these differences in teaching styles that attracted students to one teacher or another: differences in actual doctrine were minimal. For example, Mazu's best-known doctrine, "Ordinary mind is the Way," was in fact shared by all the Chan lineages:

> The Ancestor [Mazu] said to the assembly, "The Way needs no cultivation, just do not defile. What is defilement? When

with a mind of birth and death one acts in a contrived way, then everything is defilement. If one wants to know the Way directly: Ordinary Mind is the Way! What is meant by Ordinary Mind? No activity, no right or wrong, no grasping or rejecting, neither terminable nor permanent, without worldly or holy. The [*Vimalakirti*] sutra says, 'Neither the practice of ordinary people, nor the practice of sages, that is the bodhisattva's practice.' Just like now, whether walking, standing, sitting, or reclining, responding to situations and dealing with people as they come: everything is the Way."[19]

The idea expressed here—the ordinariness, or everydayness, of the ultimate truth—is found not only throughout Chan Buddhism; it is actually a Buddhist expression of the theme that we have seen repeatedly: the non-dualism of relative and absolute, or appearance and reality.

Chan is sometimes seen as anti-intellectual or anti-rational because it works on the premise that human beings are over-reliant on their rational faculties, and that more of a balance between the rational and the intuitive would be psychologically and spiritually healthy. But Chan masters themselves are often intellectuals, scholars, and philosophers who write commentaries and other books, use examples from *sutras* in their teaching, and so on. This should merely remind us that the line "not based on the written word" (in the poem attributed to Bodhidharma) refers to the mind-to-mind transmission of Chan, not to the tradition as a whole.

The Song dynasty (960–1279) saw a revival of Confucianism, known in the West as "Neo-Confucianism," which reclaimed the allegiance of most Chinese intellectuals. Nevertheless, Daoism and Buddhism continued to develop and flourish. Chan Buddhism, in particular, was integrated into the mainstream of intellectual and popular religious  life during this period. The Song was one of the high points in the history of Chinese culture, but politically and militarily it was weak, and eventually lost control of China to non-Chinese invaders.

In 1127 the nomadic Jurchen from the northeast conquered the Song capital of Kaifeng, abducting the emperor and most of the royal family. The rest of the court fled south and established a new capital in Hangzhou, while the Jurchen established their own Jin dynasty, controlling the northern half of China. This point marks the division between the Northern Song and the Southern Song. In 1234 the Jurchen were in turn conquered by the **Mongols**, whose dynasty was known as the Yuan. The Mongols proceeded to conquer the Southern Song in 1279. At this point they had assembled the largest contiguous land empire in world history, extending all the way from China to Hungary. But this enormous empire proved too far-flung to govern effectively. In 1368 the Mongols were overthrown by Chinese rebels, who established the Ming dynasty (1368–1644).

The Song was a period of active reform in politics (primarily during the Northern Song, 960–1127), education, and the economy. The power of the old aristocratic families had waned during the late Tang, and was now more centralized in the person of the emperor. Public education was widely expanded, owing in part to the invention of printing and the greater availability of books, and the civil service examination system became more important as an avenue of social mobility.

The economy came to be based mainly on money rather than trade (including paper money, for the first time in world history), and cities greatly expanded. Many of the great technological innovations that originated in China (such as movable-type printing) were made during the Song, which was also one of the high points in the history of Chinese painting, ceramics, and literature.

The Song revival of Confucianism challenged the attraction of Buddhism and Daoism among intellectuals, in part by incorporating elements of those traditions into a new synthesis that had tremendous appeal, not only in China but also in Korea and Japan. The Chan school, incorporating the Pure Land practice of chanting, came to dominate the Buddhist landscape, while Buddhist devotional piety, bodhisattvas, and Buddhas became integrated into Chinese popular religion, and new genres of Buddhist literature appeared. New sects arose in Daoism, including the Complete Perfection school, which still thrives today. In popular religion, formerly local and regional deities spread throughout much of China, in part via an improved transportation network. The Song was in many respects an exciting time in which to live in China, although overhanging it all was the persistent and ultimately successful threat of foreign domination.

Confucianism

The threat of invasion from the north and west by various nomadic peoples had been a political issue since the Han dynasty, but the Song was especially aggrieved by it. The relative affluence of China's agriculturally based economy and the cultural florescence of Chinese society since the Tang attracted border peoples desiring to trade with China, and sometimes to annex parts of it to complement their nomadic economies. The policy of the Northern Song government regarding the Jurchen was primarily to pay them off in silver in exchange for refraining from invasion, a policy that drained the treasury and ultimately failed.

Another perceived threat during the Song was an internal one. Opposition to Buddhism and Daoism had begun to arouse some Confucians in the late Tang dynasty. This movement coalesced in the eleventh century around a group of scholars who sought to reclaim the contested term Dao (Way) for what Mencius had called the "Way of the Sages" (*shengdao*). Members of this group began referring to their teachings as the "Learning of the Way" (**daoxue**), implying that neither Buddhism (the Eightfold Path or Way, *babudao*) nor Daoism (*daojiao*) understood the true Way. These scholars felt that China's social and moral fabric had been weakened by Buddhism and Daoism, and that this was contributing to its political weakness. Their movement was therefore an attempt to reassert Chinese cultural sovereignty by returning to the indigenous Confucian classics as sources of moral and political strength.

During the Northern Song (960–1127) there was considerable variety among *daoxue* scholars. But in the Southern Song (1127–1279), after the loss of North China, the term came to be used more narrowly to refer to the **Cheng–Zhu** school, named after Cheng Yi (1033–1107) and Zhu Xi (1130–1200). In the thirteenth and fourteenth centuries this school became officially sanctioned as the orthodox interpretation of Confucianism. For almost 600 years (from 1313 to 1905) this system was the basis of the civil service examination system, meaning that it had to be mastered by everyone interested in serving in government. It thus became the dominant Chinese philosophy until the twentieth century and exerted tremendous influence on all Chinese intellectuals, whether they agreed with it or not.

For many literati during these 600 years, "Neo-Confucianism" also served as a comprehensive worldview and way of life, focusing on the "ultimate transformation" of becoming a sage. It also acquired a more formal institutional setting in the form of Confucian academies, both public and private, in which the study of history, philosophy, and literature was combined with regular rituals of sacrifice to the great sages who had gone before.

Despite its origin as an opposition force to Buddhism and Daoism, Neo-Confucianism appropriated some of their important features, such as the Buddhist interest in theories of mind and the practice of meditation, and Daoist cosmology. These were subordinated, though, to the traditional Confucian goals: the moral transformation of both individuals and society. In this limited respect Neo-Confucianism was, then, a synthesis of the three canonical "Ways" of China.

The social goal was especially prominent during the Northern Song, when most of the prominent Neo-Confucians were actively involved in government and political reform. Fan Zhongyan (989–1052), for example, was a prime minister who enacted a series of political reforms aimed at rationalizing the government bureaucracy and bringing the civil service examinations more into line with the skills needed in government. Ouyang Xiu (1007–1070) wrote eloquently about the need for fundamental social reform to eliminate the underlying reasons for the popularity of Buddhism. The two most politically successful Neo-Confucians were Wang Anshi (1021–1086) and Sima Guang (1019–1086), who both served as prime minister but were bitter rivals: Sima overturned the far-reaching "New Policies" that Wang had instituted. The bitter factionalism that this represented, followed by the loss of the North to the Jurchen, soured most of the Southern Song Neo-Confucians on political reform. They therefore turned their attention inward, believing that self-cultivation was necessary before social and political reform could succeed.

In formulating their theories and methods of self-cultivation, the Song Confucians settled on Mencius as the "correct" interpreter of the original Confucian vision. They took the goodness of human nature as a premise, and devoted a great deal of attention to providing a metaphysical and cosmological basis for Mencius' theory. They also went into much greater detail outlining practical methods of self-cultivation—an area in which Mencius had been rather vague.

Neo-Confucian thought gave traditional Confucian ethics a more developed cosmological and metaphysical basis than it had before. For example, the "Western Inscription" of Zhang Zai (1020–1077) begins with a mystical vision of human nature's non-dualistic relationship with the natural world:

> Heaven is my father and Earth is my mother, and even such
> a small creature as I finds an intimate place in their midst.
> Therefore that which extends throughout the universe I
> regard as my body and that which directs the universe
> I consider as my nature. All people are my brothers and
> sisters, and all things are my companions.[1]

Zhang's phrase "that which extends throughout the universe" refers to qi, while "that which directs the universe" refers to a term that became central to Neo-Confucian thought: *li*, which means "principle" or "order" (a completely different word from the *li* that means "ritual propriety"). *Li* and *qi* became two of the most important terms in Neo-Confucian metaphysics.

Neo-Confucians also shifted the textual emphasis in the Confucian tradition away from the Five Classics. Zhu Xi proposed the "Four Books" as the core of Confucian higher education: the *Analects*, the *Mencius*, the *Great Learning* (***Daxue***), and the *Centrality and Commonality* (*Zhongyong*). The latter two were originally chapters of the *Record of Ritual* (*Liji*). Besides these, the *Yijing* (*Classic of Change*) became a major source of inspiration for the Neo-Confucian thinkers.

The *Great Learning* outlines what became the basic theory of Confucian education:

> Those in antiquity who wished to illuminate luminous virtue throughout the world would first govern their states; wishing to govern their states, they would first bring order to their families; wishing to bring order to their families, they would first cultivate their own persons; wishing to cultivate their own persons, they would first rectify their minds; wishing to rectify their minds, they would first make their thoughts sincere; wishing to make their thoughts sincere, they would first extend their knowledge. The extension of knowledge lies in the investigation of things ...
>
> From the Son of Heaven to ordinary people, all, without exception, should regard cultivating the person as the root.[2]

This presents a continuum of Confucian learning, extending from self-knowledge and moral cultivation to the practical knowledge of heading a family to the public service of governing a state. The "investigation of things" functions here to ground one's inner moral cultivation in the objective world, in order to avoid the problem of subjectivism. In other words, one's understanding of the moral order must be consistent with an objectively verifiable understanding of the natural order. These, in Neo-Confucian terms, are the two aspects of *li*: ***daoli***, the "principle of the Way" or the moral order, and ***tianli***, the "principle of Heaven" or the natural order.

Zhu Xi is the most important figure in the Confucian tradition after Confucius and Mencius. He developed core texts for an educational curriculum extending from the elementary level to what we would call graduate education, and wrote an extremely influential book on "Family Rituals."[3] Most significantly, he synthesized into a consistent whole the theories of *li* and *qi*, human nature and mind, stillness and activity, from the teachings of the Northern Song masters. The entire system is much too extensive even to summarize here,

宋
燕
國
朱
文
公
遺
像

Zhu Xi, the "synthesizer" of the Cheng–Zhu school of Neo-Confucianism. Zhu's interpretation of the Confucian tradition formed the basis of the civil service examination system from 1313 to 1905.

but what underlay it was his wish to make the pursuit of sagehood a practical endeavor for any educated person. And while he followed Mencius' general theory, he felt that Mencius had not taken sufficient account of the difficulty of achieving sagehood by cultivating and nourishing one's moral tendencies. While Mencius had focused on the goodness of human nature—now interpreted as the human endowment of *li*, the natural/moral order—Zhu Xi felt that he had not distinguished this "original nature" (**benxing**) from the "psycho-physical nature" (**qizhi zhi xing**), a term first used by Zhang Zai. The psycho-physical nature is each human being's endowment of *qi*, which clouds one's originally pure moral nature, accounting for things such as selfish desires and insensitivity to the suffering of others.

Because he deeply appreciated the difficulty of this self-transformative process, Zhu Xi went to great lengths to provide students and scholars with a structured curriculum and guidance along the way, in the form of commentaries on the classics and later works. Like

Xunzi (although for different reasons), he insisted that the ordinary person required the assistance of the sages, whose teachings were embodied in the classics.

By engaging in the lifelong pursuit of learning, aided by Zhu Xi's curriculum and commentaries, followers of the Cheng–Zhu school attempted to realize the individual goal of Confucianism: to become a sage, a transforming agent in the perfection of society. Unfortunately, the institutionalization of Zhu's thought in the civil service examination system tended to encourage rote learning and to discourage original thinking, contrary to Zhu's own dictum that learning should be "for the sake of the self."

The Cheng–Zhu school dominated Chinese intellectual life from the thirteenth century on, but never without dissent. Zhu Xi's contemporary Lu Jiuyuan (1039–1093), also known as Lu Xiangshan, differed from Zhu primarily in his view that the functioning human mind (**xin**), not just the fundamental moral nature (*xing*), is identical with principle (*li*). This led to his claim that fully understanding principle is not as difficult as Zhu Xi said; it is "easy and simple":

> Fundamentally there is nothing wanting in you. There is no need to seek elsewhere.[4]

Lu's thought was revived and expanded in the Ming dynasty (1368–1644) by one of the greatest Neo-Confucians, Wang Yangming (1472–1529). Wang too believed that the actual functioning mind is equivalent to the ultimate principle, so that we are always, in fact, conscious of what is right. Wang developed this idea in terms of the phrase from the *Great Learning*, the "extension of knowledge." While Cheng Yi and Zhu Xi had taught that this required the external "investigation of things," Wang equated it with a term used by Mencius, "innate knowledge of the good" (**liangzhi**), or moral intuition.

> The extension of knowledge is not what later scholars [the Cheng-Zhu school] understand as enriching and widening knowledge. It is simply extending one's innate knowing to the utmost (*zhi liangzhi*). This innate knowing is what Mencius meant when he said, "The sense of right and wrong is common to all human beings" [2A:6, 6A:6]. The sense of right and wrong requires no deliberation to know, nor does it depend on learning to function. This is why it is called

innate knowing. It is my nature endowed by Heaven, the original substance of my mind, naturally intelligent, shining, clear, and understanding.[5]

The differences between the Cheng–Zhu school and the **Lu–Wang** school can be summed up in terms used by Zhu Xi to describe his differences with Lu Jiuyuan. Using phrases from the *Centrality and Commonality* (section 27), Zhu said that Lu emphasized "honoring the moral nature" (***cun dexing***), while he himself emphasized "following the path of study and inquiry" (***dao wenxue***). The two phrases provide a good way of summarizing the Neo-Confucian program. Maintaining Confucius' (and Xunzi's) emphasis on learning and further developing Mencius' emphasis on cultivating and realizing one's innate moral nature—while fleshing out the philosophical basis in terms of cosmology, metaphysics, and psychology—the Neo-Confucians constructed a comprehensive worldview that has long outlasted the culture that produced it.

Neo-Confucian self-cultivation bears interesting resemblances to the realization of Buddhahood in Mahayana and Perfection (or "immortality") in Daoism. Like the bodhisattva, the Confucian *junzi* (superior person) seeks to break the habits of thinking according to individual or private (***si***) interests in favor of public (*gong*) interests. While Confucians objected to the Mahayana theory of no-self or emptiness, the original Confucian claim that individuals are inherently social beings is logically very similar to the premise of the theory of no-self, namely the radical interdependence of all things. And like the aspiring Daoist *zhenren* (perfected person), Neo-Confucians understood self-cultivation to involve the transformation of the whole person, including the psycho-physical nature.

Daoism

The major developments in Daoism after the Tang dynasty were the further development of spiritual techniques to purify the *qi* (as external alchemy was replaced by internal, or physiological, alchemy) and the growth of several new sects.

To present a sampling of Song Daoist spiritual practices we can group them according to the substances (***jing***, *qi*, or *shen*) on which they primarily focus. We saw in Chapter 4 that the three fundamental substances are associated with the three cinnabar fields of the body: *jing* (vital essence) with the lower, *qi* (vital breath) with the central, and *shen* (spirit) with the upper. The basic idea was to refine as much *qi* as possible into *shen*, and to prevent or avoid the further condensation of one's *qi* into *jing*. The following are some representative examples of techniques, starting with grossest, most physical form of *qi* and proceeding up to the purest:

(i) Nourishing the vital essence (*jing*). "Vital essence" is primarily sexual fluids, which are thought to be highly condensed forms of *qi*. Nourishing *jing* involves: (a) preserving it by interrupting sexual intercourse before orgasm and directing the *jing*, through visualization, to the highest cinnabar field (for men), or suppressing menstruation (for women); and (b) combining the male and female essences in sexual rituals, resulting in a deity called the Peach Child. These rituals, which are described in the Celestial Master texts, were rather scandalous in medieval China, and are no longer practiced. Some Shangqing texts provide instructions in meditations and visualizations that accomplish the same results in more acceptable ways.[6]

(ii) Nourishing the vital breath (*qi*). One way of nourishing the vital breath is "embryonic breathing" (***taixi***). This is based on the idea that the *qi* we are born with gradually dissipates as we age. Embryonic respiration is a means of reversing that process by clearing up blockages to the flow of *qi* through the body. Through a combination of breathing exercises and visualizations of the *qi*, one can refine the *qi* into *shen*, conceived as a spiritual "embryo," which can then leave the physical body. The stories of Daoist immortals often include their ascension to heaven. Another common means of transcending the physical body is "deliverance from the corpse" (***shijie***). In this case the subject appears to die, but afterwards the corpse in the coffin is found to be merely a staff or some other object, indicating that the body, transformed into purified *qi*, has ascended to heaven. In both these cases, the physical body is not left behind but rather transformed into a purified version of its true substance.

(iii) Nourishing the spirit (*shen*). Methods for nourishing the spirit generally involve meditation and visualization, which were very highly developed in the Shangqing school. The word *shen*, which we saw earlier meaning "gods," here refers to the most highly purified form of *qi*, which circulates in the body and accounts for sensory and intellectual knowledge. The *yin* and *yang* souls—*hun* and *po*—are forms of *shen*. In Daoist belief every person has three *hun* and seven *po* (instead of the one each that popular religion holds) and one can also synthesize more spirits from one's own *qi*. These synthesized spirits act as personal guardians and emissaries to the realm of the heavens.

Shangqing meditations include a procedure to prevent one's three *hun* from leaving the body when one is asleep, which would cause death, and a procedure to control the seven *po*, which can be troublesome even before death. Here is the method for the *hun*:

> Lie down to sleep facing upward with a pillow beneath your head, your feet extended, and your arms crossed over your heart. Close your eyes and block your breath for the space of three normal breaths, knocking your teeth three times. Envision a vermilion *qi* as large as a chicken's egg coming from within your heart and rising to emerge from between your eyes. After it emerges from between your eyes, this vermilion *qi* will become large enough to cover your body and will flow over the body to the top of your head. Transforming, it will beome fire that wraps all around your body.
>
> Once the body is encircled, cause the fire to penetrate your body as if it were igniting charcoal. Once this is complete, you should feel slightly hot internally. When this happens, again knock your teeth three times, and envisioning them, call the three *hun* by name—Bright Spirit, Embryo Light, and Tenebrous Essence—telling the three spirits to stay put.[7]

Among the new sects that arose in the Song were the two major ones that still exist today, the **Zhengyi** ("Orthodox One") sect—which claims to be the continuation of the original Way of the Celestial Masters—and the **Quanzhen** ("Complete Perfection") sect. The Zhengyi sect flourished in southern China from the twelfth century, and is still found mostly in the south and in Taiwan, where it specializes in performing rituals of healing and renewal for local communities. Quanzhen was founded in northern China by Wang Zhe, also in the twelfth century, and focuses more on individual practices such as inner alchemy. Instead of a hereditary priesthood, like the Celestial Masters and Zhengyi, its priests and practitioners are trained in monasteries. The headquarters of the Daoist Association of China today in Beijing, White Cloud Monastery (Baiyunguan), is a Quanzhen monastery.

Buddhism

Chan

It is often said that the Tang dynasty was the high point of Buddhism in China, especially Chan Buddhism. It is true that this is when the new Chinese schools began to flourish and developed their distinctively new teachings, but it was really during the Song that Buddhism thoroughly infiltrated Chinese culture. In the late Tang there had been a political repression of Buddhism, largely inspired by economic factors. Buddhist properties were tax-exempt, and so many wealthy families nominally donated extensive land-holdings to Buddhist monasteries to avoid taxes on them. In 845 the Tang emperor ordered that all Buddhist monasteries be closed and their properties confiscated by the state. This repression did not last very long, however, and institutional Buddhism bounced back fairly quickly.

Chan Buddhism fared especially well under the Song. The imperial government, believing that it would be easier to control a single sect rather than several, designated most publicly supported monasteries as Chan monasteries. In this way institutional Buddhism in China became predominantly Chan Buddhism. It was also during the Song period that Chan Buddhist teachers compiled the teachings and conversations of the great Tang masters, and thereby formulated the history of the Chan school that has been passed down through the tradition.

The practices of the Linji and Caodong lineages became more distinct during the Song, and since it was during the Song that Chan was brought to Japan, the modes of practice that developed during this period determined the shape of Zen Buddhism to this day. The most important Caodong teacher of the Song was Hongzhi Zhengjue (1091–1157), who developed the method of "silent illumination"— later reformulated as "just sitting" by the great Japanese Soto master Dogen (1200–1253)—as the core of Caodong practice. Silent illumination (*mozhao*) is an advanced form of meditation that

> involves withdrawal from exclusive focus on a particular
> sensory or mental object [such as the breath] to allow intent
> apprehension of all phenomena as a unified totality. This
> objectless meditation aims at a radical, refined non-dualism
> that does not grasp at any of the highly subtle distinctions to

which our familiar mental workings are prone and which estrange us from our experience.[8]

The most prominent Linji figure during the Song was Dahui Zong-gao (1089–1163), who popularized **gongan** (Japanese *koan*) meditation. "*Gongan*" means "public" or "legal case." In Chan usage it is a short question, or an anecdote involving one of the great Tang masters, which has no logical answer and is used as a focus of meditation. A teacher assigns a *gongan* to a student, who meditates on it until he or she comes up with a response (not necessarily an answer) that demonstrates to the teacher that a new level of enlightenment has been reached. One of the most popular *gongan* is a short dialogue between Zhaozhou Congshen (778–897) and a disciple:

> A monk asked Zhaozhou, "Does a dog have Buddha-nature?" Zhaozhou replied, "*Wu*" [which means "No," or "It does not," or "Nothing."]

What makes this dialogue useful as a *gongan* is that the answer is wrong: all sentient beings have Buddha-nature. So the student must either figure out why Zhaozhou answered in that way, or what he was intending to demonstrate with his answer, or how to show the teacher that he or she has understood and transcended the paradox. The purpose of the *gongan*, then, is to exhaust the rational mind until it allows one's intuitive enlightenment to express itself. This sudden enlightenment experience (Sanskrit *bodhi*, Chinese **wu**, Japanese *satori*) is a penetration to a deeper level of awareness that involves both the rational and the intuitive faculties.

Pure Land chanting was also combined with meditation in Chan monasteries of all lineages, from the Song through the Ming. Chanting was reinterpreted as a form of meditation, or as a form of *gongan* practice. Like those more distinctively Chan practices, chanting the name of Amitabha Buddha was understood as a means of breaking down discursive thought.

Three new genres of Buddhist literature became central to Chan during the Song: (i) the "discourse record" (**yulu**), a collection of sayings and anecdotes of a single teacher; (ii) the "lamp record" (**denglu**), a chronological collection of sayings of a series of teachers; and (iii) the *gongan* collection, a miscellaneous collection of *gongan* derived from different sources. The most popular *gongan* collections, used throughout East Asia to this day, are the **Wumen guan** (Gateless Barrier) and the **Biyanlu** (Blue Cliff Record), both compiled during the Song.

These collections of anecdotes of Chan masters and records of their conversations with students came to be as important in Chan as the older *sutras* were in other schools. Like the *Platform Sutra*, they depicted recent Chinese masters—not ancient Indian Buddhas—engaged in practice and teaching. Thus the ultimate goal of the Buddhist life, which originally had been the almost unimaginably distant goal of *nirvana*, was brought right into the sphere of everyday life.

Lay Buddhist Sects

Popular, non-scholastic, non-monastic Buddhist associations first appeared in China in around the fifth century. They were quite syncretic, sometimes borrowing elements from such non-Chinese religions as Manichaeism, which was influential during the Tang dynasty, and also from Daoism. They tended to focus on the theme of universal salvation in lay life, often mediated by a personal savior deity, such as Maitreya Buddha. This trend accelerated during the Song, as the popularity of Buddhism spread through and beyond the literati class, and continued up to the twentieth century. Song Chan masters such as Dahui preached to lay audiences in terms they could understand, and Pure Land Buddhist priests distributed the Pure Land *sutras*, engaged in public preaching, and organized congregational chanting and vegetarian meals.

The most successful lay association was the **White Lotus Society**, which became popular after the fall of the Northern Song. At this time many people were uprooted or cut off from their social ties in the north, while the new urban growth and economic developments made life more difficult for some. The White Lotus Society looked forward to the coming of Maitreya, the future Buddha, who they believed would come only after a ruler made the Dharma prevail. This element in their teachings made them a political threat, and they were at times militarily active, especially around the fall of the Yuan dynasty (1368).

Popular Religion

Two female deities rose to prominence during the Song period: the Bodhisattva Guanyin—who had earlier been portrayed as male—and the goddess Mazu (not to be confused with the Chan master Mazu). The worship of Guanyin (the male Avalokitesvara in Sanskrit), the Bodhisattva of Compassion, spread throughout China in part through the popularity of the *Lotus Sutra*, which contains a chapter devoted to the Bodhisattva. There Sakyamuni praises Guanyin as one who will grant immediate salvation to anyone who is suffering and calls on his name, and will also help in childbirth.

The process by which the iconography of Avalokitesvara/Guanyin shifted from male to female began around the tenth century and took several hundred years. Recent scholarship has suggested that the connection with childbirth may have made Guanyin especially appealing to women and stimulated her assimilation as a fertility goddess, the "White-Robed Guanyin," although other factors were also operative.[9] In any case, Guanyin became the most popular deity throughout East Asia and was incorporated into Chinese popular religion, where her identity overlapped with several other goddesses, including Mazu, who was said to have been an incarnation of Guanyin.

Mazu was a young woman, surnamed Lin, who was born in the first year of the Song dynasty and died at the age of twenty-seven, unmarried, in Meizhou, on the coast of Fujian province. According to the lore that has been passed down, toward the end of her life Mazu demonstrated special spiritual powers: she was able to help fishermen, including her father and brothers, to survive storms at sea. These powers became more evident after her death, as other seafarers reported her intervention in life-threatening storms. Thus she became known at first in her home district, after death, by the affectionate term "Auntie Lin." As her fame grew, so did her powers: eventually she could come to the aid of anyone who was in need of help. And while it is not documented, there must have been a shrine to her in Meizhou during the eleventh century.

The history of "Auntie Lin's" posthumous career is an excellent illustration of how gods are created in Chinese popular religion. It also demonstrates how local religious phenomena are co-opted or controlled by the state once they attract attention. In 1123 an imperial emissary to Korea claimed to have seen the goddess during a terrible storm on his return voyage, and credited her with his crew's ability to repair their rudder during the storm.[10] He petitioned the emperor to grant her a title, meaning that she would enter the officially approved pantheon. She was granted the first of many titles, Linghui Furen, or "Numinous Compassionate Lady."[11] In the late twelfth century an official named Hong Mai wrote about the temple to Mazu near her home:

> All merchants who are going on ocean voyages must first
> come to pray at the temple. Only when they have used
> moon blocks and asked for her protection do they dare to
> depart.[12]

Her fame and powers continued to grow, and in 1192 she was promoted to Linghui Fei, "Numinous Compassionate Imperial Consort." Around this time Mazu temples began to spread outside of Fujian province. In 1278, the Mongol emperor Kublai Khan named her Tian Fei, "Celestial Consort," and in 1409 the Ming emperor gave her the title Huguo Biminzhi Tian Fei, "Celestial Consort who Protects the Nation and Defends the People." Finally, under the Qing she was named Tianshang Shengmu, "Holy Mother in Heaven" (before 1662) and **Tian Hou**, "Empress of Heaven," in 1737. It is by these last two titles that she is still known and worshipped, mainly in southeast China and Taiwan.

Popular religion in China has for the most part always been a local affair, although certain deities, such as Guanyin and Mazu, are worshipped on regional and even national levels. As Valerie Hansen has shown, the Song was a time in which many local deities broke out of their limited territories. She describes the various kinds of deities in Song popular religion under five headings:

(i) Traditional and commoner gods, such as Mazu: those who had been historical people, with a home temple near their birthplace and branch temples elsewhere.

(ii) Buddhist, Daoist, and Confucian gods. Buddhas and Bodhisattvas (such as Guanyin) had no home temples because they were seen as more "cosmic" deities. Popular Daoist gods during the Song included **Zhenwu** or Xuanwu, an astral divinity, and **Lu Dongbin**, one of the "**Eight Immortals**." Another, with only loose connections to Daoism, was **Dongyue**, the god of the Eastern Peak, or Mount Tai in Shandong province—a sacred mountain going back to the Han dynasty. Chief among the Confucian deities was, of course, Confucius.

(iii) Generic or bureaucratic gods. These include local earth gods (*tudi shen*, today called *tudi gong*) and city gods (*chenghuang shen*), who usually have personal names but are referred to by their offices, which may be filled by different deities over time, usually eminent deceased residents or officials. Another type of generic god is the dragon, which is similar to the earth god except it inhabits local bodies of water, and is prayed to especially in times of drought.

(iv) Animal and nature gods, such as rivers and mountains, were very common in ancient times but were dying out by the Song (except for important mountains such as Dongyue).

(v) Regional gods, such as Zitong, originally from Sichuan, who helped aspiring officials pass the civil service examinations, and eventually became Wenchang, the national god of exams. Mazu could be placed into this group as well as the first one.[13]

State Religion

At this point it is useful to introduce a pair of analytical categories that were first proposed by the sociologist C.K. Yang: "institutional" and "diffused" religion.[14] The difference between the two relates to the social setting in which religion is practiced. Institutional religion is religion that is practiced in social institutions that are specifically and uniquely religious, such as a church or a monastery. Diffused religion is religion practiced in "secular" social settings such as the family, the community, and the state. Ancestor worship, for example, is diffused religion because it is practiced solely within the family and involves no representatives of specifically religious institutions, such as priests or monks.

Popular religion is for the most part, but not entirely, diffused. Temples might be considered religious institutions, and Daoist priests often officiate at public rituals in temples. However, local temples that are not affiliated with the Buddhist or Daoist establishments are financed and operated by ordinary community members, and many rituals are performed by community officials who have no institutional religious affiliation or by ordinary community members elected each year to officiate.

An important ministry of the imperial government was the Bureau of Rites (**Libu**), which governed an elaborate schedule of rituals conducted by government officials, from the emperor on down. The most important of these was the annual sacrifice to Heaven on the winter solstice, performed by the emperor in a sumptuous ritual involving hundreds of people. This was one of the two annual "great sacrifices," the other being the sacrifice to Earth on the summer solstice. There were also "middle sacrifices" made to local gods, to the sun and moon, to wind and rain, to previous emperors, and to Confucius. The "minor sacrifices" included those to Guangong (god of war), to Wenchang, and to the city god.

The sacrifice to Heaven was an extremely grand and elaborate ceremony that took place on the Altar of Heaven (***Tiantan***), just south of the imperial palace in Beijing, which became the capital during the Yuan dynasty. The Altar of Heaven is a large, open, circular, three-level platform surrounded by a square enclosure. All its architectural elements have numerological significance in terms of correlative cosmology, many of them based on the correspondence of odd numbers with *yang* and even numbers with *yin*. The altar is the southernmost ritual structure on a north–south axis along which the large imperial retinue would march from the palace. The northernmost structure is the "Hall for Prayer for the Year" (***Jiniandian***), where the emperor would would stop first to pray for a good harvest. This is the large, circular, three-tiered building today commonly called the "Temple of Heaven." Next is a similar but smaller structure, one story high, in which the emperor would perform sacrifices to his ancestors.

The Altar of Heaven (Tiantan) in Beijing. This is the southernmost of a series of ritual structures at which the Chinese emperors performed the most important annual sacrifices of the state religion.

Finally he would come to the Altar of Heaven, where at midnight on the winter solstice he would sacrifice livestock to his symbolic father, Heaven.

The significance of the winter solstice lies in the fact that this is the point in the year when *yin* is at its highest point and *yang* at its lowest, when the sun at noon is at its lowest point of the year. This is the turning point, when the sun begins to rise higher in the sky each day at noon, when the *yang* forces in the cosmos begin to increase again, eventually to reach their peak on the summer solstice. The function of the emperor at this moment, and at the corresponding moment on the summer solstice, was to facilitate the *yin–yang* fluctuation of cosmic forces by ritually enacting his filial role as "Son of Heaven." In this ritual—which occurred up through the first decade of the twentieth century—the Chinese ruler was playing the same key role as were the Shang kings in 1300 B.C.E. when, through frequent sacrifice and divination, they acted as the crucial linkage or pivot between Heaven and Earth.

These state rituals ended when the last dynasty fell, in 1911. Since then, the Republic of China (on the mainland until 1949, and since then in Taiwan) has preserved only a vestige of the state cult: the sacrifice to Confucius on his birthday, September 28, in the government-supported Confucian temples in the major cities. But popular religion on the level of the family and the local community is still practiced.

Western Religions in China

All the major religions of Western Asia had begun to enter China by the Tang dynasty, when the Silk Routes were heavily traveled. These included Zoroastrianism (the highly dualistic Persian religion), Manichaeism (combining elements of Zoroastrianism, Christianity, and Buddhism), Judaism, Christianity, and Islam. Zoroastrianism never extended beyond the expatriate Persian community, and after the 845 suppression of Buddhism (which also included foreign religions) it never regained a foothold. Manichaeism (named after the third-century Persian prophet Mani) was popular among the **Uighurs** of western China (along with Buddhism), but it was eventually absorbed into Buddhist and Daoist sects, while the Uighurs became almost exclusively Muslim. Judaism thrived in Kaifeng, the capital of the Northern

Song dynasty: a synagogue was built in 1163, with permission from the emperor, and a Jewish community lasted there until the early twentieth century, although the synagogue disappeared in the late nineteenth century. There were other Jewish communities in Ningbo, Hangzhou, and Guangzhou. The Jews in China were never singled out for persecution (aside from occasional repressions of all foreign religions), but the communities have gradually been assimilated to the point where their descendants today may be aware of their Jewish heritage but know nothing about Judaism.

The two most successful "Western" religions in China were Islam and, to a much lesser degree, Christianity. Islam was introduced in 651, when the third caliph sent tribute to the Tang emperor to promote trade along the Silk Routes. From then on Arab traders traveled to China both by land and by sea, and were given residences in Chang'an and several cities along the coast. Mosques and cemeteries soon followed. Between the tenth and the twelfth centuries, Islamic expansionism caused frequent warfare in Central Asia. This ended temporarily when the Mongols controlled the whole region, during which period (the Yuan dynasty) many Muslims also settled in northwest and southwest China. But after the Mongol empire collapsed in the late fourteenth century the warfare continued, and by the end of the Ming dynasty (early seventeenth century), ten ethnic minorities in western China were largely Muslim.

The earliest form of Christianity in China was the **Nestorian sect** (founded by the fifth-century Bishop of Constantinople, Nestorius, and later declared heretical by the Vatican), which entered shortly after Islam. Alopen, a Nestorian missionary from Persia, was received by the Tang emperor in 635 and built a church in Chang'an. It was banned along with the Buddhist suppression in 845, although it was reintroduced from Mongolia in the thirteenth century.

During the Yuan dynasty Dominican and Franciscan missionaries established a presence in China under the Mongol Khans, but this lasted only about a century. The next wave of Christian missionary activity came when the Jesuits arrived in China in the late sixteenth century. The most influential Jesuit missionary was Matteo Ricci (1552–1610), an Italian priest who settled in Beijing. Ricci became very learned in Chinese, even to the point of writing books in the language. He became part of the intellectual community in Beijing and was a valued adviser to the imperial court on such topics as cartography and astronomy.

The Jesuits had considerable success making converts, especially among the literati, and gained approximately 150,000 converts by 1650. The key to their success was that they tolerated their flock's continued practice of ancestor worship and state religious rituals. If they had demanded that Chinese Christians give up these practices it is unlikely that they would have had much success at all. This tolerance (or "accommodation"), though, was based on the view that these were not really religious rituals (in Christian terms), because they did not involve worship of the Supreme Being, whom the Jesuits identified as Shangdi (the Lord on High). They argued, for instance, that ancestor worship was merely a way of honoring the ancestors. Thus they were at the same time broad-minded in their cultural attitudes and exclusivistic in their definition of religion.

This paradox led to a prolonged conflict known as the "Rites Controversy" within the Catholic Church, and eventually to the Church's banishment from China. The conflict began when Dominican and Franciscan missionaries came to China in the late seventeenth century and opposed the Jesuit accommodations for ancestor worship. They saw ancestor worship and the other rituals as genuine religious phenomena. But this meant that they were, in their eyes, idolatry and superstition. They accordingly protested to the Pope that Chinese converts should not be allowed to continue these practices, and in 1704 the Pope ruled against the Jesuits. In 1706 the Chinese expelled all missionaries except those who agreed to ignore the papal decree. In 1724 all churches outside Beijing were closed, many of them destroyed, and Catholic missionaries were restricted to Guangdong (Canton) and Macao. In 1773 the Jesuit order was outlawed entirely in China, ending the first successful wave of Christian missionary activity in China.

In the nineteenth century, however, as Spanish and Portuguese sea power declined, the British, Dutch, and Americans became the dominant players in the China trade. The traders were often accompanied by Protestant missionaries, who established themselves first in the southeastern coastal cities, where they are still the strongest. These missionaries played important roles in China's modernization, for example by leading the opposition to footbinding, and by establishing schools and hospitals.

<table>
<tr><td>Modern China</td><td>6</td></tr>
</table>

Modern China | 6

The Qing dynasty fell in 1911, ending the era of imperial China after more than 2000 years. The Republic of China, which took its place, led by the Nationalist Party (**Guomindang**) of Sun Yat-sen (1866–1925), was weak and plagued by corruption. In 1921 the Chinese Communist Party was founded, and after a brief period of  cooperation with the Guomindang, now led by Chiang Kai-shek (1887–1975), the two parties began a civil war for control of China. The Communist Party was led by Mao Zedong (1893–1976).

After the Second World War, during which the Nationalists and Communists cooperated against their common enemy the Japanese, the Communists quickly gained the upper hand and forced the Nationalists to retreat to the island of Taiwan. On October 1, 1949, Mao Zedong proclaimed the founding of the People's Republic of China. Since then there have been, in effect, two Chinas: the People's Republic of China on the mainland, and the old Republic of China on Taiwan.

On the mainland, Communist ideology requires atheism, or opposition to religion, as official policy. The suppression of religion began in the 1950s, but reached its peak during the tumultuous Cultural Revolution, from 1966 to Mao Zedong's death in 1976. Most temples were destroyed, and those that were spared were converted to such non-religious uses as army barracks or warehouses. Confucianism was the most harshly attacked tradition, because it was associated with all that had been wrong with the "old China." The People's Republic stood for a "new China," which its leaders understood to be based on the "scientific" principles of Marxism and Maoism.

After Mao's death, the more pragmatic Deng Xiaoping came to power in 1979 and opened up China to the West and to limited forms of market capitalism. The restrictions on religion were relaxed, and from 1980 many temples were rehabilitated. The constitution of the People's Republic guarantees freedom of religion, as long as one refrains from proselytization. There are five officially sanctioned religions: Buddhism, Daoism, Islam, Protestant Christianity, and Catholic Christianity. Confucianism is not considered a religion at all, but it too has been partially rehabilitated—at least to the extent of allowing scholars to study it. Popular religion falls under the official category of "superstition" (*mixin*) and is not supported, but since about 1990 there has been something of a revival of popular religion despite government policy. The revival is especially strong in the southeast, where Taiwanese tourists and pilgrims have contributed money to rebuild temples, especially those of Mazu. In Taiwan religion for the most part has never been suppressed.

The New Confucians

Just as its validity was questioned after the fall of the Han dynasty, so Confucianism was discredited by the complete collapse of the imperial system in the early twentieth century. Although there had always been innovation throughout the history of the tradition, cultural conservatism was built into its value system, and this was not popular when the Republic was striving to modernize. Still, there were philosophers who sought to modernize Confucianism rather than abandon it completely.

One of the most influential of these thinkers was Xiong Shili (1885–1968), who was strongly influenced by Buddhism. Xiong, a group of his students, and their students became known as the "New Confucians." A slightly younger contemporary of Xiong's, Feng Youlan (1895–1990), was also very influential and may be included in this group. Feng's greatest influence, however, was as a historian of Chinese philosophy, while Xiong's was through his students.

Among those students and followers were Tang Junyi (1909–1978), Mou Zongsan (1909–1994), and Xu Fuguan (1903–1982), all of whom settled in Taiwan and Hong Kong. In 1958 Tang, Mou, Xu, and Zhang Junmai (also called Carsun Chang, 1886–1969) together published *A Manifesto for a Re-appraisal of Sinology and Reconstruction of Chinese Culture*, a bold statement of the claim that Chinese culture, and particularly Confucianism, had something to offer to philosophy and religion in global perspective.[1] This served as an

announcement to the scholarly world at large that a new generation of Confucian scholars was on the scene.

The third generation of New Confucians includes those still active
today, such as Tu Weiming, Liu Shu-hsien, and Cheng Chung-ying.[2]
These scholars, unlike their predecessors, have trained a generation of Western scholars (and ethnically Asian scholars educated in
the West) who, if not explicitly identifying themselves as Confucians,
have continued their work. All of these scholars share the basic premises
that Confucianism has not been adequately understood in the contemporary world, that it may in fact have something to offer to
comparative religious philosophy, and that modernization of the
tradition requires separating out those elements that are inextricably
wedded to aspects of Chinese culture that are no longer considered
tenable (such as the subservience of women) from those that are applic-
able in a modern liberal-democratic setting.

While a growing number of mainland Chinese scholars are
sympathetic to this view, the majority—indoctrinated to believe that
Confucianism is an "idealist" and "feudal" system—tend to be amused
and incredulous at the growing Western interest in Confucianism.

Daoism and Popular Religion

One of the distinctive features of medieval Daoist religion was the
sharp differentiation of its heavens, its gods, and its practices from
their "lower" analogues in the popular religion. Daoist deities occupied the three highest of the nine heavens; they were true emanations
of the Dao rather than the spirits of ordinary people or natural objects,
and their worship never demanded the sacrifice of live animals. But
once the earliest Daoist communities, under the Celestial Masters,
became more integrated into Chinese society (after their forced relo-
cation in 215), their religious practices began to absorb elements of
popular religion.

Today, most of those who call themselves Daoists are Daoist priests,
monks, and nuns (the latter two in the Complete Perfection sect),
along with some lay practitioners at Daoist temples and monasteries.
The most common setting in which non-Daoists come into contact
with Daoism is when they attend public or private rituals at local temples. Although most of these temples have no institutional affiliation
with Daoism, Buddhism, or Confucianism, the priests who perform

the rituals are usually Daoist priests, hired by individuals, families, or communities to perform specific rituals, either in a home or at a community temple. Thus Daoism has become, to some extent, integrated with popular religion, although it maintains a separate institutional identity.

The Spiritual World

Chinese popular religion is a dynamic, localized system which adapts to changing social factors through time and from place to place. It is therefore difficult to summarize, but there are certain commonalities. One of these is the division of the spiritual world into gods, ghosts, and ancestors, none of which is ontologically distinct from living human beings: all four groups are manifestations of *qi*, and all follow the same natural principles. While they each have their own Way (*dao*)—the ideal pattern or path they should follow—and there is of course a difference between the realm of the living (*yang*) and that of the dead (the *yin*, dark, or "occult"), all four groups are part of the natural order. Thus, in a sense, there is no "supernatural," strictly speaking, in Chinese religion.

Another aspect of this non-dualistic worldview harks back to correlative cosmology. The tripartite division of gods, ghosts, and ancestors parallels the social distinction of government officials, "beggars and bandits," and family members. These distinctions and correspondences are evident in numerous ways.

GODS (*SHEN*) There are two types of gods in Chinese popular religion: *fu* are the spirits of charismatic people, or what Valerie Hansen has called "traditional and commoner gods"; ***shi*** are "officials," or "generic or bureaucratic gods" in Hansen's list.[3] *Fu* gods include cultural heroes (such as the mythic Yellow Emperor [Huangdi], Confucius, and Mazu) and military heroes (such as the god of war, Guandi). Some say today that Mao Zedong is in the process of becoming a god. Any of these gods may have a temple or altar devoted to them, and in mainland China, local gods—and not only Mazu—are becoming popular again, even without government recognition and support.[4]

Shi or bureaucratic gods—like officials among the living—are in most cases temporary occupants of a position. These include local earth gods (*tudi gong*—"*gong*" meaning "official"), city gods (*chenghuang shen*), the kitchen god in a household (**Zaojun**, Lord of the Stove), and, at the top of the bureaucratic hierarchy, the

A woman worshipping Mazu at Longshan Temple, Taibei. Behind her are tables for sacrificial offerings and in front of her is a large incense pot. The image of the goddess is inside the structure just visible in the right rear.

Jade Emperor (**Yuhuang Dadi** or Yuhuang Shangdi), also called the Lord of Heaven (Tiangong). Some of these, especially city gods, may previously have been ancestors.

City gods always have their own temples, while earth gods usually just have small shrines in public places and altars in larger temples; individual families may also have the local earth god on their family altars, with their ancestors. The kitchen and other household gods, of course, are found only in homes, in the form of an image either on paper affixed to the wall or a statuette on a shelf. The Jade Emperor does not have many temples, because—like the human emperor—he is seldom approached directly by ordinary people, who prefer to deal with lower officials, as they more readily accept gifts in exchange for favors.

All of these "officials" hold positions in the spiritual bureaucracy, modeled after the old imperial bureaucracy. The position of city god corresponds with the local magistrate, the lowest level in the imperial bureaucracy, while the earth god corresponds roughly to the local officer appointed by the magistrate. Magistrates were men who had passed the highest level of civil service exams and were assigned, on a rotating basis, by the imperial government. As the sole local representative of the emperor—never in their home districts— their role combined the executive (including police) and judicial functions of government in a local district, roughly corresponding to counties today.

GHOSTS (*GUI*) A ghost is the spirit of a deceased person who has no family to conduct ancestor worship, or whose death was irregular in some way—for example, if the body was lost at sea. Ghosts are discontented souls or the neglected dead: spirits who lack proper roles in the social network and so are socially marginal, like the "beggars and bandits" with whom they are often compared. Ghosts are both dangerous and pitiful, and so people make offerings to them—again, as one would give something to a beggar. Offerings to ghosts are always made outside the house, and always outside the back door. During a major festival with Buddhist origins, the "Ghost-feeding Festival" in the seventh lunar month, or August (equivalent to *O-bon* in Japan), a large community feast is prepared for wandering ghosts and living beggars.

The spirits of unmarried women—such as Mazu—are particularly prone to become ghosts, because women normally become part of their husbands' family lines and are not worshipped as ancestors by their natal families. In Mazu's case, she quickly began to be worshipped as a god, so the danger of her becoming a ghost was averted. In ordinary cases there are various ways of doing this. The natal family might set up a separate altar just for her, or conduct a "spirit marriage," marrying her off either to an unmarried deceased man, or to a living man who agrees to take her on as a second "wife." This allows her to become an ancestor in another family, just as she would have had she been married. Spirit marriage is quite common in Taiwan today.[5]

ANCESTORS (*ZU*, OR *ZUXIAN*) Becoming an ancestor is a ritual process, requiring a proper funeral that includes certain specific rituals. Either a Daoist or a Buddhist priest may conduct a funeral, and there are usually elements of both religions in the liturgy. For example, in a Daoist funeral the priest may send a messenger (in the form of a small image that is burnt) to the underworld carrying a writ of pardon for the deceased, to be delivered to the Ten Kings of Hell (a Buddhist element) so that the spirit may quickly ascend to Heaven instead of spending time in Hell being punished for his or her transgressions. In the same ritual, a symbolic elixir of immortality (Daoist) may be applied to the lips of an effigy of the deceased, which is then burnt.[6]

Ancestor worship has been called the most fundamental form of Chinese religion. Dating back at least to the religion of the Shang kings, it is still practiced today, especially in Taiwan. Most Taiwanese families have an altar table—colloquially called the "red table"—holding images and name plaques for both ancestors and gods. Ritual offerings may be made every morning, or weekly, or only on special occasions, such as birthdays. These offerings include the burning of incense and an offering of fresh fruit or cooked rice. The ancestors on a family altar usually go back only two or three generations, including those who were known personally by living members. When name plaques are retired they are ritually burnt; it is thought that the ancestor's *qi* gradually disperses when offerings are no longer made. Some families have an ancestral or family temple (*jiamiao*), containing a large altar cabinet with name plaques of ancestors going back many generations. This may be within an extended family compound, or in the case of a village where most residents share a single surname, in a public location.

The question often arises whether ancestor worship would not be more accurately described as "ancestor veneration," something fundamentally different from the worship of a god. However, the ritual actions performed before gods and ancestors are basically identical. A family altar table always holds both ancestors and gods, and there is little distinction made between them in the worship ritual. And as we have seen, the distinctions among gods, ghosts, and ancestors are fluid: ancestors can become either gods or ghosts.

The most significant difference between gods and ancestors can be described from two perspectives. The phenomenological distinction—the "emic" or insider's understanding—is that gods have more numinous power (**ling**) than ancestors, and can therefore influence a community wider than just a single family. The way this is determined is through dreams and spirit-possession. From this flows the sociological distinction—the "etic" or outsider's understanding—that ancestors are worshipped by only a single family (whether nuclear or extended), while gods are worshipped by a larger community. Both gods and ancestors can be appealed to for protection, but neither group is omnipotent or totally benevolent. Gods may be jealous of their power, and ancestors may take revenge on living family members for insults or slights.

Gods and ancestors are both *yang* phenomena (deriving from the *hun*, or *yang* soul). Ghosts, on the other hand, are *yin* (deriving from the *po*) and always cause trouble. While ancestors generally affect only their own family, they sometimes cause trouble for another. In that case, the one family's ancestor is, to the other family, a ghost.

Ritual

The main ritual elements in popular Chinese religion may be conceived as ways of interacting with spiritual beings: sacrifice, divination, and exorcism. Except for certain elaborate community rituals, sacrifice today consists merely in offerings of fruit or other food items. In the home it is usually fruit for either gods or ancestors, or cooked rice (in a bowl with chopsticks, and perhaps with condiments) for ancestors—just as if they were living relatives sharing the meal. It is conceived as sustenance for the ancestor, who imbibes the spiritual vapors of the food.

In temples, offerings to the gods usually consist of fruit or packaged food items. Fully prepared food is never offered to gods, whether in the home or in temples; in some cases it may be cooked, but then it is neither seasoned nor sliced. To offer fully prepared food to a god would be presumptuous, as it would be the equivalent of sharing the meal with someone of equal social status. This would be out of harmony with the natural/social order or Dao, and would have unfortunate repercussions. Ghosts may be offered cooked food, but never in the house: a small table is set outside the back door.

Spirit money is also burnt for gods, ghosts, and ancestors. Gods should be given gold (usually just rough paper bills with some gold foil), ancestors are given silver, and ghosts copper. Many temples have large ovens outside the main gate for this purpose, as do small earth-god shrines. Every fifteen days business owners in Taiwan burn spirit money in red braziers and set out offering tables on the sidewalk for both gods and ghosts. This follows an ancient calendrical system divided into twenty-four fifteen-day periods. Some of the offering tables are quite elaborate; for example a restaurant may offer an entire meal, complete with beer or wine.

On the surface all these gifts—especially the money—may appear to be nothing more than "bribes" to spiritual officials, but there is also a deeper principle: that of mutual obligations. In Confucian terms, this is the principle of reciprocity (*shu*), one of the more important virtues discussed in the *Analects*. This, in turn, is based on a more fundamental aspect of the Chinese worldview: the assumption that things are defined by their relationships with other things. Gift exchange in Chinese society is the mechanism by which these relationships are affirmed, maintained, and strengthened. And so it is only natural that the same mechanism be used to maintain relationships with gods and ancestors. One further implication is that there are obligations on both sides. When a god is treated correctly and yet fails to improve the life of the petitioner, one is entitled to find another god. Conversely, to experience good fortune and fail to express gratitude to the gods is an invitation to disaster. Ancestors have presumably already made their contributions during their lifetimes, so one does not normally expect favors from them. One always has a debt to one's ancestors, and sacrifice is repayment.

Divination today commonly takes four forms: moon blocks (*bei* in Mandarin, *poe* in Taiwanese), divination slips (*qian*/*chiamm*), spirit-mediums (*jitong* or *tongji*/*dangki*), and divination chairs or palanquins (*jiao-a*/*kio-a*).[7] Moon blocks are by far the most commonly used, especially in temples, and are sometimes used in conjunction with divination slips. Spirit-mediums, or shamans, are used both for divination and to manifest the presence of a god during temple festivals or rituals. Some spirit-mediums in Taiwan have storefront offices in cities, but they can also be consulted at temples or brought into homes, and they may be either men or women. Those who participate in community rituals or temple festivals are usually young men who, in trance, cut their chests and backs with knives or flails, drawing considerable blood, to show that they are under the control of the god—since no one in his right mind would do that to himself of his own will. Among other reasons, self-mutilation is considered highly unfilial, as it shows disrespect to the parents who gave you your body.[8] When a shaman performs as a diviner, he or she self-induces a trance, for example by rocking back and forth on a bench and chanting for twenty minutes or so. Attendants then lead the shaman to the client, who asks specific questions, and the shaman's replies are written down by the attendants. After the session (and also after the self-mutilation at a festival), the shaman disconnects him- or herself from the god by jumping backward and being caught by attendants. It is spirit-mediums who most often identify the source of a problem, such as a particular ancestor or god. Appearances in dreams or visions are also means of identification. The divination chair, or palanquin (sedan chair), is a miniature chair, perhaps eighteen inches high, that is regarded as a seat for the deity. It is held by two people, each holding two legs, who go into a sort of semi-trance and shake the chair up and down rhythmically. At some moment, together, they spontaneously bend the chair over and, with one of the arms of the chair, trace out on a tabletop some Chinese characters. These are read and recorded by someone sitting at the table, and are regarded as a written response to the question brought by the client. Sometimes a spirit-medium is also present to draw the deity into the chair.

Exorcism of troublesome ghosts is usually performed by a kind of Daoist priest known as a "red-hat" (as opposed to the more orthodox and more highly trained "black-hat") priest. The red-hat priests are an example of the partial fusion of Daoism and popular religion. They are not necessarily trained in the canonical Daoist scriptures and rituals, and perform only those rituals that do not require extensive scriptural knowledge.

Some rituals are organized and paid for by entire communities, such as the Ghost-Feeding Festival. One of the most elaborate public rituals is called the *Jiao*, a "rite of cosmic renewal" for a community that takes place over several days and involves every family in a village or community, several Daoist priests, ritual theatrical performances, sacrifice of live pigs (contrary to the Daoist disdain of this practice), and a huge community feast.[9] This expensive ritual is only performed about once a generation, or even at intervals of up to sixty years.

All temples have birthday celebrations for their resident gods. These are sponsored by community associations and run by either local officials or community members chosen, on a rotating basis each year, for the job. In these respects this is therefore "diffused" religion, since no religious professionals are involved—although the temple itself may be considered a religious institution, and a Daoist priest may be hired to perform specific rituals during the festival. The birthday celebration itself involves taking the image or images of the god out in a palanquin (today often carried on the back of a small truck) in a procession through the village or city neighborhood. This is the equivalent of the "inspection tour" conducted by a magistrate or higher official, and occasionally the emperor himself, in imperial times. The procession is often a long parade, with musicians, dancers, children's groups, firecrackers to scare away ghosts, and people in large costumes representing other gods who are congratulating the temple god on his or her birthday.

Another major festival is more associated with Confucianism than Daoism or Buddhism: the **Qingming** ("clear and bright") festival in early spring, commonly known as Tomb-sweeping Day. This takes place 105 days after the winter solstice, when vegetation is beginning to grow again and the *yang* principle is returning. In villages there may be a traditional theatrical performance, performed outdoors for the local gods—especially the earth god, who is ritually invited to attend and escorted, in a covered palanquin, to the site. The most important part of the festival is family gatherings in cemeteries, where they clear their ancestors' tombs, explode firecrackers to scare away ghosts, burn incense and pray to the ancestors, and usually have a family group photograph taken. It is not so much a mourning ritual as a family reunion, including both living and deceased members, and it shows again the permeability of the boundary between the social and spiritual worlds, and the importance of the family in constructing individual identity in Chinese society.

The Dao of Popular Religion

The foci of Chinese popular religion today are chiefly the family and the local community (village or city neighborhood). The function of most popular religious practice is the maintenance of harmony (**he**) within the social network and between the social and spiritual realms. For example, if there is a dispute between two families, rather than engage lawyers and courts, people typically use spirit-mediums, or the gods they speak for, as intermediaries. Spirit-mediums and fortune-tellers are also used for personal and family problems. A local spirit-medium who is familiar with the parties involved and local history may be able, consciously or unconsciously, to suggest solutions that are acceptable to both sides. This, of course, is an "etic" description of what might be occurring; the "emic" equivalent would be that a god actually intervenes.

The case of spirit marriage also illustrates the underlying conception of the Dao of popular religion. The premise here is that the ideal family is one in which all offspring live to adulthood, marry, die natural deaths, have proper funerals, and are properly worshipped as ancestors. When breaches in this ideal order occur, it must be repaired, and that involves ritual.

Another situation that requires a ritual solution is the absence of male children to continue a family's descent line. In such a case an unrelated male is adopted, usually a younger brother from another family, who does not have primary responsibility to continue his own descent line. He then agrees to place the ancestors of the childless couple—and the couple when they die—on his family altar table. If he was adopted as an adult, they and their ancestors may share the altar with his own ancestors. The purpose of this sort of adoption, as well as spirit marriage, is to ensure everyone a place in the ancestral-social system. This ideal social order, comprising the living, the dead, gods, and ghosts, is the Dao of Chinese popular religion.

A Buddhist Revival

Attempts to modernize Chinese Buddhism began in the late nineteenth century with the reformer Yang Wenhui (1837–1911). Yang, a Buddhist layman, believed that Buddhism was potentially compatible with Western science, and that by building on this compatibility Buddhism could be spread to Western civilization. Yang and others stressed Buddhist rationalism by attempting to rid the tradition of its more superstitious elements, and by engaging in social work. One of these reformers was the Abbot Taixu (1890–1947), who in 1915 developed a plan for "The Reorganization of the Sangha," which stressed the need for Buddhist social activism outside the monastery, including hospitals, orphanages, and modern schools combining Buddhist and secular education. Although his plan was never implemented in China, it may be considered the forerunner of "engaged Buddhism," a mode of Buddhist practice based on social action, which has become increasingly popular both in Asia and the West.[10] Taixu's term for this was "Buddhism for life in this world." As Whalen Lai has put it:

> It was Venerable Taixu who brought Buddhism out of the cloisters into the modern world, who revived the Mahayana commitment to working in the world, who directed Buddhist reflection to current social issues, and who, during the national emergency facing China at the time, encouraged Buddhists, even monks, to participate actively in national defense.[11]

One of Taixu's students was Yin-shun (b. 1906), who became probably the leading Chinese Buddhist intellectual of the twentieth century. Yin-shun, who later moved to Taiwan, has written a number of scholarly studies in which he develops "a Mahayana bodhisattvic recommitment to living in the here and now."[12] This inspired the fastest-growing Buddhist movement in the Chinese cultural sphere today: the **Tzu Chi** (Compassion Relief) Foundation in Taiwan.

Tzu Chi was founded as a charitable organization in 1966 in Hualien, Taiwan, by the Buddhist nun Cheng Yen (b. 1937), a student of Yinshun. She and about thirty others, mostly housewives, vowed to set aside half a New Taiwan dollar (equivalent at that time to about U.S. 1.3¢) each day for a fund to aid poor families. During the first year they distributed about $435; today the Tzu Chi Foundation claims to have dispersed about U.S.$68 million and to have about 5 million members worldwide (mostly in Taiwan).

Tzu Chi's social mission is focused on charity, medicine, education, and culture. The foundation has become especially proficient at providing disaster relief after typhoons, floods, and earthquakes, both in Taiwan and other parts of Asia, including mainland China. After the serious earthquake in Taiwan on September 21, 1999, Tzu Chi relief workers did most of the early rescue work as government officials dithered over who had jurisdiction. Tzu Chi has built and runs a hospital, a College of Medicine, and a College of Nursing, and they have plans for kindergartens, elementary and secondary schools, and a university. The educational philosophy of these Tzu Chi institutions is primarily Buddhist:

> Features of the curriculum at the college [of medicine] include getting a good education, nurturing the spirit of humanitarianism, and building up correct perspectives on life and morality. Humanitarianism is an attitude toward life and a cultivation of humanity. The goal of Tzu Chi education is not competition for high grades, but the activation of humanity's deep, pure buddha nature, love and compassion.[13]

Zen meditation is part of the curriculum, but there are also Western elements, and at the College of Nursing the traditional Japanese arts of the cultured woman—tea ceremony and flower arranging—are taught.[14]

Although the teachings and works of Taixu, Yin-shun, and Cheng Yen have no doubt been influenced by Christian charitable work, they are also the direct heir to the Mahayana Bodhisattva's Vow, Nagarjuna's insistence that emptiness does not mean nothingness, the Chinese ideal of the bodhisattva who "enters the marketplace with a helping hand"[15] (which in turn is probably influenced by the Confucian ideal of the sage who transforms society), and the Chan master Mazu's dictum "Ordinary mind is the Way." In other words, the social work of the Tzu Chi Foundation is Chinese Buddhist practice through and through.

The Future of Chinese Religion

There are five officially recognized religions in mainland China today: Buddhism, Daoism, Protestant Christianity, Catholic Christianity, and Islam; popular religion is regarded as "superstition" and Confucianism as an "ideology," and both of these categories are considered to be mutually exclusive of religion. The Chinese constitution guarantees freedom of religious belief, as long as it does not undermine the Communist Party or the government: for example, preachers cannot hold services at unregistered locations or use unauthorized books or tapes. Each of the five recognized religions has a bureaucratic link to the government (for example, the Buddhist Association of China, the Daoist Association of China) through which government control is exerted. The legal restrictions, however, have become harder and harder to enforce, especially with Christianity and popular religion, while Buddhism and Islam have been troublesome for the government because of their connections with smouldering resentment and nascent independence movements in Xinjiang (the far-western Uighur Special Administrative Region) and Tibet.[16]

Another major issue for the future of Chinese religions in the People's Republic arises from the nearly complete disenchantment with the Marxist/Maoist worldview and the resulting moral and spiritual vacuum. The Tiananmen massacre of June 4, 1989, may have confirmed the demise of the official worldview, although its obsolescence began to be evident with the introduction of market capitalism in the 1980s. It has become increasingly clear that, despite the rhetorical focus on "the people" (*min*), the Chinese Communist Party does not trust the people of China. Yet after the nearly complete destruction of the old China—especially its Confucian socio-ethical fabric and the patchwork quilt of popular religion—the "New China" (*Xinhua*) has failed to provide the people with a lasting source of socio-ethical values. It tried to replace the family as the basic social unit with the collective farm or work-unit (*danwei*), only to give that up in the 1980s. To forge a collective, national identity in the global community it has relied largely on century-old feelings of victimhood, but it remains to be seen whether this alone can sustain a healthy sense of national identity far into the twenty-first century.

The people of mainland China are in the meantime turning in growing numbers to Christianity and popular religion for a worldview that fills the spiritual vacuum. The only form of officially recognized Catholicism is the Catholic Patriotic Association, which is controlled by the government and has no ties to the Vatican. Yet, many Chinese continue to be loyal to the Roman Catholic Church and often meet clandestinely. Protestants also meet in illegal "house churches." Periodic clampdowns on such illegal forms of religious practice make religious life in mainland China rather tense, yet the number of Christians continues to grow rapidly—recent estimates suggest perhaps 20 million Protestants and 10 million Catholics. Still, that is only about 1.2 percent of the population.

Popular religion has far more potential in China than Christianity. Apart from the mainland revival of worship of popular deities, such as Mazu, and the building of many new temples, there has also been a great deal of interest in **qigong**, which is primarily rooted in Daoist religious practice. *Qigong* means "exercise (or manipulation) of *qi*," and refers to a huge number of eclectic practices—from **Taijichuan**, which has a fairly long history, to new forms that seem to crop up every year. The best-known of these in the West is, of course, **Falun gong**.

Falun gong is the creation of Li Hongzhi (b. 1951 or 1952), who now lives in the United States. The name means "Exercise of the Dharma Wheel" (a circle of *qi* that the adept can manipulate through meditative hand motions), and its doctrine is constructed in primarily Buddhist terms. The organization founded by Li in 1992 is called **Falun Dafa**, or "Great Dharma (or Law) of the Dharma Wheel." It came to international attention when an estimated 10,000 followers staged a silent sit-in outside the residence compound of China's top leaders in Beijing on April 25, 1999, to protest what they said was a slanderous magazine article and the refusal of the authorities to let them register as a religious organization. The demonstration was right next to Tiananmen Square, and was pulled off without any prior knowledge of the state security police. This showed that Falun Dafa had the capability to mobilize large numbers of people under the direction of a leader who was outside the government's control. It is largely for this reason that the government quickly outlawed the sect and began a harsh campaign of repression that is still ongoing. Although the doctrines of Falun gong are rather unusual, on the whole they are no more unorthodox than many other *qigong* groups.

The situations of Falun gong and Christianity illustrate the dilemma of religion in mainland China today. The government of the People's Republic is obsessed with control and fearful of dissent, yet it recognizes that religion cannot be wiped out and that the Chinese economy needs at least a certain amount of market capitalism, which works against centralized control.[17] This means that the future of religion in mainland China very much depends on the future of the present system of government. Many people believe that the economic liberalization that China has enjoyed since the 1980s will eventually lead to political liberalization, which is roughly what happened in Taiwan and South Korea.[18]

It is in the nature of liberal democracy to allow, even to encourage, a "spiritual marketplace" of ideas. The burgeoning Western scholarship on Chinese religions over the past forty years is making available to a huge new audience some very new ways of understanding and experiencing the world. Some Chinese religious and philosophical concepts (such as *yin* and *yang*, *qi*, *dao*) have already entered the English lexicon. Many Westerners are disenchanted with their biblically based religions and find Buddhism, Daoism, or Confucianism appealing. Ideas such as interdependence and compassion in Buddhism, the Daoist view of the body as a spiritual microcosm, the Confucian belief that human nature is good and that humans are primarily social beings—all of these often find sympathetic ears in Western classrooms.

Western attraction to non-Western ideas goes back to ancient Greece's fascination with Egypt. And it is a story with tragic possibilities, if we succumb to the temptation to exoticize and objectify the other, using the other simply as a foil to define ourselves in idealized terms.[19] But we are aware of that danger now, and those interested in Chinese (or any other) culture should strive to avoid it. Whether or not that is possible, Chinese religious ideas and practices are likely to continue to infiltrate Western cultures, just as Western culture has infiltrated China since at least the nineteenth century. Thus the future of Chinese religions, in the long run, may not be limited to China.

Notes

Chapter 1

1 The swastika is an ancient Indian symbol that was co-opted by the Nazis as part of their fraudulent claim to represent the "Aryan" civilization. The Aryans were the civilization that migrated from western Asia into both Greece and India in the second millennium B.C.E. The earliest teachings of Buddhism, the "Four Noble Truths," are actually called the "Four Aryan Truths." The swastika in India actually predates the Aryans.

Chapter 2

1 The "Shang" of "Shang Di" is not the dynastic name; it is merely a homonym meaning "high" or "above."

2 David N. Keightley, *Sources of Shang History: The Oracle Bone Inscriptions of Bronze Age China* (Berkeley: University of California Press, 1978), pp. 33–35, 222. The divination procedure described below is also from Keightley, chapters 1–2.

3 Mu-chou Poo, *In Search of Personal Welfare: A View of Ancient Chinese Religion* (Albany: State University of New York Press, 1998), chapters 3–4, relying in part on newly discovered Zhou dynasty "daybooks" (*rishu*), the early progenitors of Chinese almanacs.

4 Translated by Mu-chou Poo, *In Search of Personal Welfare*, p. 37. See the next chapter for a description of the *Classic of Odes*.

5 Mu-chou Poo, p. 83.

6 Mu-chou Poo, pp. 39–40.

Chapter 3

1 This is a form of the "problem of theodicy," a term that originally referred to the problem in the biblical traditions: How is it that evil exists if God is supremely good and supremely powerful? A question or dilemma like this—basically inquiring into the nature and cause of evil and suffering—lies at the heart of every religio-philosophical tradition.

2 Trans. Irene Bloom, in Wm. Theodore de Bary and Irene Bloom, eds, *Sources of Chinese Tradition*, 2nd edn (New York: Columbia University Press, 1999), vol. 1, chapter 3. For the convenience of the reader, all translations in this book (unless otherwise noted) are from vol. 1 of the 2nd edition of *Sources*. In the case of the *Analects*, the Chinese edition upon which this translation is based differs slightly in passage numbering from most other recent translations. Where that is the case, the alternate passage number is given after a slash.

3 Trans. Arthur Waley, *The Analects of Confucius* (1938; rpt. New York: Knopf, 2000).

4 Bloom's translation has "That he would react accordingly" here (p. 129), but this is not in the Chinese text.

5 *Understanding Religious Life*, 3rd ed. (Belmont: Wadsworth, 1985), p. 2.

6 My translation.

7 Trans. Irene Bloom, *Sources*, p. 334.

8 Ibid., p. 338, with "authentic" substituted for "sincere" (*cheng*).

9 Trans. D.C. Lau, *Lao Tzu: Tao Te Ching* (London: Penguin Books, 1963).

10 These and subsequent passages trans. D.C. Lau.

11 See also *Laozi* 4, "The Way is vacuous."

12 See Harold D. Roth, "The Inner Cultivation Tradition of Early Daoism," in Donald S. Lopez, Jr., ed., *Religions of China in Practice* (Princeton: Princeton University Press, 1996), pp. 123–4.

13 Trans. Victor H. Mair, *Wandering on the Way: Early Taoist Tales and Parables of Chuang Tzu* (1994; rpt. Honolulu: University of Hawaii Press, 1998), p. 130–31.

14 Mair, p. 158. See also *Laozi* 37:
The Way is constant: by doing nothing, nothing is left undone.
If lords and kings can hold to it, all things will, of themselves, be transformed (*zihua*).

15 Trans. adapted by Irene Bloom from Wing-tsit Chan, in *Sources*, p. 387. Guo Xiang is discussing the next to last section of *Zhuangzi*, chapter 2 (dialogue between Penumbra and Shadow; see Mair, p. 24).

16 Mair, p. 59. "The Great Clod" is one of Zhuangzi's humorous names for the Dao.

17 Mair, pp. 168–9. The word for "destiny," *ming*, is the same as the word for "mandate" or "decree" in "Mandate of Heaven" (*tianming*). In both cases it means something like "what is given," or that which we have no control over. In popular usage it means "destiny" or "fate," as in one's allotted lifespan, but for Zhuangzi it is not that deterministic.

18 Mair, p. 16.

19 *Sources*, p. 100 (editors' comment).

20 Zhuangzi tells of this happening to him at the end of his chapter 2.

21 Mair, p. 22.

22 Ibid., pp. 15–16.

23 Trans. Burton Watson, *Sources*, p. 106, slightly modified.

24 Mair, p. 71.

25 Ibid., p. 35.

26 Ibid., p. 184.

27 *Sources*, pp. 110–111. Note that here Confucius is back in the role of the fool (becoming the disciple of his own student), as also in the next quotation.

28 Mair, p. 182.

Chapter 4

1 The twenty-eight lunar lodges were a system of marking out the year, similar to the twelve constellations of the zodiac. Horn was the first and Axletree was the last.

2 *Springs and Autumns of Mr. Lü*, trans. Nathan Sivin, in *Sources*, p. 239.

3 *Commentary on the Appended Phrases* [of the *Yijing*], trans. Richard John Lynn, in *Sources*, p. 320. The *Yijing* is composed of sixty-four hexagrams, or six-line diagrams, each of which is a pair of three-line "trigrams," of which there are eight. The hexagrams each have a name reflecting the overall *yin–yang* structure, and each is thought to represent an "archetype" of a social or natural situation in which the diviner can be involved. They are attributed to the first mythic sage, Fuxi. It is impossible to determine an actual date of origin, although they may very well go back to the beginning of the Zhou dynasty in the eleventh century B.C.E., or even earlier. The trigrams and hexagrams are composed of solid lines, symbolizing *yang*, and broken lines, symbolizing *yin*. The Eight Trigrams and their primary symbolic associations are:

☰ Qian (Heaven)   ☱ Dui (Lake)
☲ Li (Fire)   ☳ Zhen (Thunder)
☷ Kun (Earth)   ☶ Gen (Mountain)
☵ Kan (Water)   ☴ Sun (Wind)

4 Ibid., p. 329, except for the first sentence, which is my translation. For a complete translation see Mary Lelia Makra, trans., *The Hsiao Ching* (New York: St. John's University Press, 1961).

5 See D.C. Lau, *Mencius*, appendix 2.

6 *Sources*, pp. 821–4.

7 Ibid., pp. 822–3.

8 Trans. Burton Watson, in *Sources*, p. 584.

9 For one of the relevant sections of the *Guanzi* (mid-fourth century B.C.E.), see *Sources*, pp. 256–63. In 1973 another collection of Huang-Lao texts was discovered in a 168 B.C.E. tomb outside the village of Mawangdui, near the city of Changsha in Hunan province. These silk manuscripts have been tentatively identified as the long-lost *Four Classics of the Yellow Emperor*. See *Sources*, pp. 241–56. Along with these texts, the cache included two editions of the *Laozi*—older than the standard edition handed down until then—an older edition of the *Yijing*, and some medical texts, among others.

10 See Livia Kohn, "Laozi: Ancient Philosopher, Master of Immortality, and God," in Lopez, *Religions of China in Practice*, pp. 52–63.

11 See Stephen R. Bokenkamp, *Early Daoist Scriptures* (Berkeley: University of California Press, 1997).

12 Stephen R. Bokenkamp, "Sources of the Ling-pao Scriptures," in Michel Strickmann, ed., *Tantric and Taoist Studies*, vol. 2 (Brussels, 1983), pp. 434–86. According to Bokenkamp, it is possible that Ge Chaofu's inspiration for this new development was the fact that some Shangqing material suggested that his ancestor Ge Xuan had not advanced very far in the realm of the immortals. So Ge Chaofu was defending the honor of his family, which was a well-entrenched part of the southern aristocracy, against that of the *arriviste* Xu's (pp. 442–3).

13 Livia Kohn, *Daoism and Chinese Culture* (Cambridge, MA: Three Pines Press, 2001), p. 91.

14 From Du Guangting (850–933), *Yongcheng jixian lu* (Records of the Assembled Transcendents of the Fortified Walled City), trans. Suzanne Cahill, "Pien Tung-hsüan: A Taoist Woman Saint of the T'ang Dynasty (618–907)," in Arvind Sharma, ed., *Women Saints in World Religions* (Albany: State University of New York Press, 2000), p. 215.

15 These words are in Sanskrit, the classical or literary language of ancient India, which is part of the same Indo-European language family as are the Germanic and Romance languages, including English.

16 It should be noted that the Chinese word for the Buddhist concept of emptiness, *kong*, is not the same as the word used in the *Laozi*, which is *xu*, or "vacuity."

17 In this section I will occasionally refer to Japanese Zen and include Japanese equivalents for Chinese words when they are more familiar to Western readers.

18 William F. Powell, *The Record of Tung-shan* (Honolulu: University of Hawaii Press, 1986), p. 2.

19 Nelson Foster and Jack Shoemaker, eds, *The Roaring Stream: A New Zen Reader* (Hopewell, NJ: Ecco Press, 1996), p. 45.

Chapter 5

1 Trans. Wing-tsit Chan, in *Sources*, p. 683.

2 Trans. Irene Bloom, in *Sources*, pp. 330–31.

3 See *Sources*, pp. 737–44, 803–4, 812–13.

4 Trans. adapted from Wing-tsit Chan, in *Sources*, p. 718.

5 Ibid., p. 846.

6 Bokenkamp, *Early Daoist Scriptures*, pp. 275–372.

7 Trans. Bokenkamp, ibid., p. 323, substituting *hun* for "cloudsoul" and *qi* for "pneuma."

8 Taigen Daniel Leighton with Yi Wu (trans.), *Cultivating the Empty Field: The Silent Illumination of Zen Master Hongzhi* (San Francisco: North Point, 1991), p. xv.

9 See Chün-fang Yü, *Kuan-yin: The Chinese Transformation of Avalokitesvara* (New York: Columbia University Press, 2001).

10 See Valerie Hansen, *Changing Gods in Medieval China, 1127–1276*

(Princeton: Princeton University Press, 1990), p. 33.

11 See James L. Watson, "Standardizing the Gods: The Promotion of T'ien Hou ('Empress of Heaven') along the South China Coast, 960–1960," in David Johnson, Andrew J. Nathan, and Evelyn S. Rawski, eds, *Popular Culture in Late Imperial China* (Berkeley: University of California Press, 1985), pp. 292–324.

12 Quoted in Hansen, p. 145.

13 Ibid., pp. 180–83.

14 C.K. Yang, *Religion in Chinese Society* (Berkeley: University of California Press, 1961).

Chapter 6

1 Translated in Carsun Chang, *The Development of Neo-Confucian Thought*, vol. 2 (New York: Bookman, 1962), appendix. For an abridged version, see de Bary and Lufrano, *Sources of Chinese Tradition*, 2nd ed., vol. 2, pp. 550–58.

2 While not usually included in the "New Confucian" category, Wing-tsit Chan (1901–1994) and Wm. Theodore de Bary, who is still active, have also been instrumental in reviving interest in Confucianism, especially in the United States.

3 See Arthur P. Wolf, "Gods, Ghosts, and Ancestors," in Wolf, ed., *Religion and Ritual in Chinese Society* (Stanford: Standford University Press, 1974), pp. 131–82.

4 See, for example, Kenneth Dean's article about Guo Chongfu (963–976), who died as a child and is worshipped in Fujian province as Guo Shengwang (Saintly King Guo) or Guangze Zunwang (Reverent Lord of Broad Compassion): "Daoist Ritual in Contemporary Southeast China," in Lopez, *Religions of China in Practice*, pp. 306–26.

5 See David K. Jordan, *Gods, Ghosts, and Ancestors: Folk Religion in a Taiwanese Village* (Berkeley: University of California Press, 1972),

pp. 140–54.

6 See the film *Taoism: A Question of Balance*, part of the series The Long Search, produced by the BBC in the 1970s.

7 See Jordan, *Gods, Ghosts, and Ancestors*, chapter 4.

8 There are exceptions to this rule: when a parent is mortally ill, a traditionally accepted response is to cut off a piece of one's own flesh and boil it in a broth for the parent. Living flesh was thought to be powerfully curative, since it still contains the *yang* life principle. This was, in fact, the highest possible act of filiality in premodern times, and often figures in stories of the gods, as in one of the manifestations of Guanyin, Princess Miao-shan. See Chün-fang Yü, "The Cult of Kuan-yin in Ming-Ch'ing China," in Irene Bloom and Joshua A. Fogel, eds, *Meeting of Minds: Intellectual and Religious Interaction in East Asian Traditions of Thought* (New York: Columbia University Press, 1997), pp. 144–74.

9 See Michael Saso, *Taoism and the Rite of Cosmic Renewal*, 2nd ed. (Pullman: Washington State University Press, 1990).

10 The term "engaged Buddhism" was coined by the Vietnamese Zen master Thich Nhat Hanh, who is probably the second best-known Buddhist monk (after the Dalai Lama) in the world today.

11 "Introduction" to *The Way to Buddhahood: Instructions from a Modern Chinese Master*, by Venerable Yin-shun (Boston: Wisdom Publications, 1998), p. xx.

12 Ibid.

13 "Tzu Chi College of Medicine: Tzu Chi Education Mission," http://www.tzuchi.org/global/about/missions/education/index.html.

14 "Tzu Chi College of Nursing: Tzu Chi Education Mission," http://www.tzuchi.org/global/about/missions/education/index.html.

15 This is the title of the last of the

"Ten Oxherding Pictures," a series of drawings illustrating the path of the Bodhisattva, attributed to the twelfth-century Chinese Chan master Guoan.

16 Both of these were formerly called "autonomous regions," although that name was changed because they actually demanded some autonomy.

17 The official Marxist/Maoist rationale for allowing religion to exist is that religion will not become extinct until the social conditions that produce it—inequality and class conflict—disappear. The aim of Communism is to reach that state, but until that happens religion must be tolerated.

18 The political and religious situations in Taiwan are, of course, very different from the mainland. Despite the fact of a rather inglorious recent past (martial law until 1987, government-controlled media, repression of dissent, police massacres of native Taiwanese), Taiwan has recently become the first full democracy in Chinese history.

19 A process often called "orientalism," after Edward Said's book by that title.

Glossary

I have used the *pinyin* system of transliteration throughout the text. Wade-Giles equivalents are given below in parentheses.

Amituo (A-mi-t'o) The **Buddha** Amitabha, whose vows are the basis for **Pure Land** Buddhism.

anatman [Sanskrit] "No-self" or "no-soul," a central doctrine in Buddhism, denying the reality of any independent, unchanging, autonomous selfhood.

Avatamsaka Sutra [Sanskrit]/*Huayanjing* (*Hua-yen-ching*) "Flower Garland Sutra," central text of **Huayan** Buddhism.

Baopuzi (*Pao-p'u-tzu*) The "Master Who Embraces Simplicity," the Daoist alchemist Ge Hong (283–343), and the title of the book he wrote.

bei (*pei*) [Taiwanese *poe*] Divination blocks (or "moon blocks"), the most common form of **divination** in popular religion.

benxing (*pen-hsing*) "Original (moral) nature" in Neo-Confucianism.

Biyanlu (*Pi-yen lu*) *Blue Cliff Record*, one of the most popular *kongan* (*koan*) collections in **Chan** (Zen) Buddhism.

bodhi [Sanskrit]/*wu* Enlightenment in Buddhism.

bodhisattva [Sanskrit]/*pusa* (*p'u-sa*) Buddhist enlightened being who vows to remain in *samsara* to help other sentient beings attain enlightenment.

Buddha [Sanskrit]/Fuo (Fo) An "awakened one," either the historical Sakyamuni Buddha or one of many others in **Mahayana** Buddhism.

Caodong (Ts'ao-Tung) One of the major lineages in **Chan** Buddhism (Japanese Soto).

Celestial Masters Orthodox Daoist sect founded by Zhang Daoling in 142 C.E.

Chan (Ch'an) One of the new schools of Chinese Buddhism (Japanese Zen).

channa (*ch'an-na*) Transliteration of *dhyana* [Sanskrit] or "meditation," origin of the name of the **Chan** school of Buddhism.

Cheng–Zhu (Ch'eng–Chu) Dominant school of Neo-Confucianism, named for Cheng Yi (eleventh century) and Zhu Xi (twelfth century).

cheng huang (*ch'eng-huang*) City god in popular religion.

chuan (*ch'uan*) To transmit or hand down.

cun dexing (*ts'un te-hsing*) "Honoring the moral nature" in Neo-Confucianism.

dan (*tan*) Elixir, alchemy.

dantian (*tan-t'ien*) "Elixir field," one of three spiritual centers of the human body in Daoism.

dao (*tao*) The Way or Path.

dao wenxue (*tao wen-hsüeh*) "Following the path of study and inquiry" in Neo-Confucianism.

Daodejing (*Tao-te ching*) Daoist classic attributed to the mythical Laozi.

Daojia (*Tao-chia*) Classical Daoism.

Daojiao (*Tao-chiao*) The Daoist religion, or ecclesiastical Daoism.

daoli (*tao-li*) Principle of the Way, or moral principle/order in Neo-Confucianism.

daoshi (*tao-shih*) Daoist master.

daoxue (*tao-hsüeh*) "Learning of the Way," a term for Neo-Confucianism.

Daozang (*Tao-tsang*) The Daoist Canon.

Daxue (*Ta-hsüeh*) The *Great Learning*, one of the "Four Books" in Confucianism.

de (*te*) Moral power/potential in Confucianism; the power inherent in things in Daoism.

denglu (*teng-lu*) "Lamp record," a collection of hagiographical stories of teachers in a particular lineage of **Chan** Buddhism.

Dharma [Sanskrit]/*fa* The teachings, truth, or law of the **Buddha**.

Di Lord, god.

Diamond Sutra One of the *Prajña-paramita* (Perfection of Wisdom) *sutras* in **Mahayana** Buddhism.

divination Obtaining answers to specific questions through non-empirical means, for example from gods or ancestors.

Dongyue (Tung-yüeh) God of Mount Tai, one of the sacred mountains of China.

Eight Immortals Legendary historical figures who became gods in Daoism and popular religion.

emptiness [*kong* (*k'ung*), Sanskrit *sunyatta*] Central doctrine in **Mahayana** Buddhism [Sanskrit *sunyatta*], stating that all things lack independent, autonomous, self-nature.

Falun dafa (Fa-lun ta-fa) Great Law of the Dharma Wheel, aka **Falun gong**.

Falun gong (Fa-lun kung) Dharma Wheel Exercise, the eclectic *qigong* practice founded by Li Hongzhi in 1992 and banned in 1999.

fu Gods who were formerly human beings.

gong (*kung*) Public, official, duke, god.

gongan (*kung-an*) [Japanese *koan*] "Public case," a brief anecdote or statement by a former **Chan** master, used as a focus of meditation.

Guandi (Kuan-ti)/Guangong (Kuan-kung) God of war and business, the former Guan Yu (third century C.E.).

Guanyin (Kuan-yin) [Sanskrit Avalokitesvara] The **Bodhisattva** of Compassion in **Mahayana** Buddhism.

gui (*kuei*) Ghost.

Guomindang (Kuo-min-tang) Nationalist Party, founded by Sun Yat-sen.

he (*ho*) Harmony.

Heart Sutra One of the most influential *Prajña-paramita* (Perfection of Wisdom) *sutras* in **Mahayana** Buddhism.

Hinayana "Lesser Vehicle," a pejorative term coined by adherents of **Mahayana** Buddhism to refer to the **Theravada** and other earlier schools.

hua Transformation.

Huainanzi (*Huai-nan-tzu*) A Huang-Lao Daoist text of the second century B.C.E.

Huangdi (Huang-ti) The mythic Yellow Emperor.

Huang-Lao Eclectic form of Daoism (named after Huangdi and Laozi), followed by the early Han dynasty court until the adoption of Confucianism in 136 B.C.E.

Huayan (Hua-yen) [Sanskrit *Avatamsaka*] "Flower Garland", one of the new schools of Chinese Buddhism.

Huineng (638–713) The Sixth Patriarch of **Chan** Buddhism.

hun The *yang*-soul.

Jiao (Chiao) Ritual of community renewal.

jiao-a (*chiao-a*) [Taiwanese *kio-a*] Palanquin or chair divination.

jing (*ching*) Essence, one of the three fundamental forms of *qi* in the Daoist conception of the body.

jing (*ching*) Classic, scripture, *sutra*.

Jiniandian (*Chi-nien-tien*) Hall for Prayer for the Year, sometimes called Temple of Heaven.

jitong (*chi-t'ung*)/tongji (*t'ung-chi*) [Taiwanese *dangki*] Spirit-medium, shaman.

junzi (*chün-tzu*) "Superior person" in Confucianism.

karma Buddhist theory of moral causality.

kun (k'un) Earth trigram/hexagram of the *Yijing*.

Laozi (*Lao-tzu*) Early Daoist classic, named after the mythic figure Lao Tzu (the Old Master); also called the *Daodejing* (Classic of the Way and its Power).

li Principle, order.

li Ritual, ritual propriety.

liangzhi (*liang-chih*) Innate knowledge of the good in Confucianism.

libationer [*jijiu* (*chi-chiu*)] The chief priest of a Daoist community in the Celestial Master sect.

Libu (*Li-pu*) Bureau of Rites.

Liji (*Li-chi*) *Record of Ritual*, one of the Five Confucian Classics.

ling Numinous power.

Lingbao (Ling-pao) Numinous Jewel, one of the textual traditions of Daoism.

Linji (Lin-chi) [Japanese Rinzai] One of the major lineages in **Chan** Buddhism.

Loshana Vairocana, the cosmic **Buddha**.

Lotus Sutra Central text of **Tiantai** Buddhism.

Lu Dongbin (Lü Tung-pin) Chief of the **Eight Immortals**.

Lu–Wang School of Neo-Confucianism, named after Lu Jiuyuan (twelfth century) and Wang Yangming (sixteenth century).

Lunyu (*Lun-yü*) *Analects* of Confucius, one of the "Four Books" in Confucianism.

Mahayana "Greater Vehicle," the branch of Buddhism that spread throughout East Asia.

Maoshan Mt. Mao, near Nanjing, center of Shangqing tradition of Daoism.

Mazu (Ma-tsu) Most popular deity in Taiwan, patron deity of seafaring people.

Mengzi (*Meng-tzu*) *Mencius*, one of the "Four Books" in Confucianism.

Mile (Mi-lo) Maitreya, **Buddha** of the Future.

min The people, masses.

ming Clear, bright.

minjian zongjiao (*min-chien tsung-chiao*) Popular religion.

mixin (*mi-hsin*) Superstition.

mofa "End of the Dharma," the final period of the current cosmic epoch in Buddhism, in which people are no longer able to achieve enlightenment.

Mongols Nomadic culture that conquered northern China in 1127 and the rest in 1279; established Yuan dynasty.

Nagarjuna Influential Indian **Mahayana** philosopher (second century C.E.).

Nanwu Amituofo (Nan-wu A-mi-t'o-fo) "Homage to Amitabha Buddha," the *mantra* chanted in **Pure Land** Buddhism.

neidan (*nei-tan*) Internal (physiological) alchemy in Daoism.

Nestorian Christianity The earliest Christian sect to enter China, in the seventh century.

nianfo (*nien-fo*) The act of chanting the **Buddha**'s name.

nirvana The extinguishing of the karmic causation leading to rebirth in Buddhism.

non-dualism A way of thinking, characteristic of Chinese thought, in which differences are real but are parts of a more fundamental unity.

parinirvana "Complete *nirvana*," with no ensuing rebirth, at the death of a **Buddha**.

Platform Sutra Central text of **Chan** Buddhism, attributed to Hui-neng (638–713).

po (*p'o*) The *yin*-soul.

Pure Land [*jingtu* (*ching-t'u*)] [Sanskrit Sukhavati] The celestial paradise into which followers of **Pure Land** Buddhism hope to be reborn.

qi (*ch'i*) Psycho-physical-spiritual substance, the stuff of which all existing things are composed.

qian (*ch'ien*) [Taiwanese *chiamm*] **Divination** slips in a Chinese temple.

qian (ch'ien) Heaven trigram/hexagram of the *Yijing*.

qigong (*ch'i-kung*) Manipulation or exercise of *qi*.

qing (*ch'ing*) Feeling, disposition.

Qingming (*Ch'ing-ming*) "Clear and Bright," spring festival, also called Tomb-sweeping Day.

qizhi zhi xing (*ch'i-chih chih hsing*) "Psycho-physical nature" in Neo-Confucianism.

Quanzhen (Ch'üan-chen) "Complete Perfection" school of Daoism, founded by Wang Zhe in the Song dynasty.

Qufu (Ch'ü-fu) Birthplace of Confucius.

Qunqiu (*Ch'un-ch'iu*) *Spring and Autumn Annals*, one of the Five Confucian Classics.

ren (*jen*) Humanity/humaneness, the cardinal virtue in Confucianism.

ren xing (*jen-hsing*) Human nature.

ren zheng (*jen-cheng*) Humane government.

ru (*ju*) Scholar, Confucian.

sacrifice Offering to a deity.

samsara The cycle of birth, death, and rebirth in Buddhism.

Sangha The Buddhist community of monks, nuns, laymen, and laywomen.

sanjiao (*san-chiao*) "Three Teachings,"—Confucianism, Daoism, and Buddhism.

Sanqing (San-ch'ing) "Three Pure Ones," highest Daoist deities.

Sanyi (San-i) "Three Ones," Daoist deities residing in the human body.

Shang Di (Shang Ti) High Lord.

Shangqing (Shang-ch'ing) "Highest Purity" heaven and textual tradition in Daoism.

shen Spirit, god.

sheng Sage.

shi (*shih*) Literati, scholar-officials, bureaucratic gods.

Shijiamouni (Shih-chia mou-ni)/Shijia (Shih-chia) Sakyamuni **Buddha.**

shijie (*shih-chieh*) "Deliverance from the corpse" (ascension to immortality) in Daoism.

Shijing (*Shih-ching*) *Classic of Odes*, one of the Five Confucian Classics.

shu Reciprocity, a Confucian virtue.

Shujing (*Shu-ching*) *Classic of Documents*, one of the Five Confucian Classics.

si (*ssu*) Private.

sutra Buddhist sacred text containing the discourses of the **Buddha.**

Taijichuan (*Tai-chi ch'uan*) Supreme Polarity Exercise.

Taiqing (*T'ai-ch'ing*) "Most Pure" heaven and textual tradition in Daoism.

Taishang (*T'ai-shang*) "Most High" heaven and textual tradition in Daoism.

Taishang Laojun (T'ai-shang Lao-chün) Lord Lao the Most High, source of the revelations to the **Celestial Masters** of Daoism.

taixi (*t'ai-hsi*) Embryonic breathing, form of Daoist meditation.

Theravada "Way of the Elders," the sole surviving school (*nikaya*) of several that flourished before the development of **Mahayana**; now found in South and Southeast Asia.

Three Jewels [*Sanbao*] The **Buddha,** the *Dharma,* and the *Sangha.*

Tian (*T'ien*) Heaven.

Tian Hou (T'ien-hou) Empress of Heaven, the goddess **Mazu.**

tian ren heyi (*t'ien-jen ho-i*) "Heaven and humanity are one," a Chinese proverb.

tiandao (*t'ian-tao*) Way of Heaven.

tianli (*t'ien-li*) Principle of Heaven, or natural principle/order in Neo-Confucianism.

tianming (*t'ien-ming*) Mandate of Heaven in Confucianism.

Tianshang Shengmu (T'ien-shang Sheng-mu) Holy Mother in Heaven, the goddess **Mazu.**

Tianshidao (T'ien-shih-tao) Way of the **Celestial Masters** in Daoism.

Tiantai (T'ian-t'ai) One of the new Chinese schools of Buddhism.

Tiantan (*T'ien-t'an*) Altar of Heaven in Beijing, site of the emperor's annual sacrifice to Heaven.

tudi gong (*t'u-ti kung*) Local earth god.

Tzu Chi Buddhist Compassion Relief Foundation, based in Taiwan, founded in 1966 by the nun Cheng Yen.

Uighur Turkic-speaking Islamic culture, mainly in the far western province of Xinjiang.

Vajrayana "Diamond Vehicle," or Tantric Buddhism, found primarily in Tibet, Mongolia, and Manchuria.

waidan (*wai-tan*) External (laboratory) alchemy in Daoism.

wang King.

wei "Artifice" for Laozi; for Xunzi, "consciously created."

wen Literature, culture.

Wenchang (Wen-ch'ang) God of examinations.

Wenshu Manjusri, **Bodhisattva** of Wisdom.

White Lotus Society Lay Buddhist movement popular from twelfth to nineteenth centuries.

wu Enlightenment, *bodhi, satori* in Buddhism.

wu jing (*wu-ching*) Five Classics in Confucianism.

Wumen guan (*Wu-men kuan*) *Gateless Barrier*, one of the most popular *gongan* (*koan*) collections in **Chan** [Zen] Buddhism.

wuwei (*wu-wei*) "No doing"; absence of no deliberate, goal-directed action.

wuxing (*wu-hsing*) Five Phases (water, fire, wood, earth, and metal) in Chinese cosmology.

xian (*hsien*) Daoist immortal.

xiangfa (*hsiang-fa*) "Pseudo **Dharma**," the middle period of the current cosmic epoch in Buddhism, in which only a few people are capable of achieving enlightenment.

xiao (*hsiao*) Filial devotion, a Confucian virtue.

Xiaojing (*Hsiao-ching*) *Classic of Filiality*, an influential Confucian text.

xin (*hsin*) Honesty, faithfulfulness—a Confucian virtue.

xin (*hsin*) Mind/heart.

xing (*hsing*) The nature (of a thing).

Xinhua (Hsin-hua) New China.

xinzhai (*hsing-chai*) "Fasting of the mind," a practice recommended by **Zhuangzi**.

Xiongnu (Hsiung-nu) A nomadic tribe that repeatedly challenged the northern borders of China.

xu (*hsü*) Vacuity, emptiness in Daoism.

xue (*hsüeh*) Learning.

Yellow Springs Early Chinese conception of the afterlife.

Yijing (*I-ching*) *Classic of Change*, one of the Five Confucian Classics, also used in Daoism.

yin-yang "Dark–light," passive–active, contracting–expanding, a basic principle in Chinese thought.

Yuhuang dadi (Yü-huang ta-ti)/Yuhuang shangdi (Yü-huang Shang-ti) Jade Emperor, the highest deity in the pantheon of popular religion.

yulu (*yü-lu*) Discourse record, a collection of sayings by a **Chan** Buddhist master; a genre later adopted by Neo-Confucianism.

Zaojun (Tsao chün) Stove god in popular religion.

zheng (*cheng*) To oppose, argue, contend.

zhengfa (*cheng-fa*) "Correct **Dharma**," the first period of the current cosmic epoch in Buddhism, when people could hear and understand the Buddha's teachings directly.

Zhengyi (Cheng-i) "Orthodox One" school of Daoism, which claims to be the continuation of the early **Celestial Masters** tradition.

zhenren (*chen-jen*) "Perfected Person" in Daoism.

zhenru (*chen-ju*) "True suchness," a term for the ultimate principle of emptiness in **Tiantai** Buddhism.

Zhenwu (Chen-wu)/Xuanwu (Hsüan-wu) A Daoist astral deity.

zhi (*chih*) Wisdom.

zhong (*chung*) Loyalty, a Confucian virtue.

Zhongyong (*Chung-yung*) *Centrality and Commonality* (or *The Mean*), one of the "Four Books" in Confucianism.

Zhuangzi (*Chuang-tzu*) The second major text in classical Daoism, named after its main author, Zhuang Zhou (Chuang Chou; fourth century B.C.E.).

zihua (*tzu-hua*) Self-transformation.

ziran (*tzu-jan*) Natural, spontaneous.

zu (*tsu*)/**zuxian** (*tsu-hsien*) Ancestor.

zuochan (*tso-ch'an*) Sitting meditation [Japanese *zazen*] in **Chan** Buddhism.

zuowang (*tso-wang*) Sitting and forgetting, a form of meditation recommended by **Zhuangzi**.

Pronunciation Guide

The *pinyin* system of romanization has been used for Chinese names and terms in this book. The most glaring differences between this system and standard English pronunciation are the following:

c is pronounced something like ts
q: ch
x: sh
zh: j
shi: sher
zhi: jer
ri: ruh
zi: ʤə
other final i: ee
final e: uh (for example, de: duh; le: luh)

Above and in the following list, the standard phonetic symbols ə (unaccented vowel) and ʤ (dz as in adze) have been used.

Amituo: ah-mee-taw
bei: bay
benxing: bən-shing
Bian Dongxuan: byen dong-shwan
Caodong: tsow-dung
Caoshan: tsow-shan
Chang'an: chahng-ahn
Cheng Chung-ying: chəng jong-ying
Chi: cher
chuan: chwan
cun dexing: tsun duh-shing
Dahui Zonggao: dah-hway ʤung-gow
Damo: dah-maw
dao: dow
dao wenxue: dow won-shweh
Daojia: dow-jyah
Daojiao: dow-jyow
daoli: dow-lee
daoshi: dow-sher
daoxue: dow-shweh
Daxue: dah-shweh

de: duh
Deng Xiaoping: dung shyow-ping
Di: dee
Dongyue: dong-yueh
Faxian: fah-shyen
Feng Youlan: fung yo-lan
Fuxi: foo-shee
gongan: gong-ahn
Guandi: gwan-dee
Guangting: gwahng-ting
Guangzhou: gwahng-jo
Guanyin: gwan-yin
gui: gway
Guo Xiang: gwaw shyahng
Guomindang: gwaw-min-dahng
Han: hahn
Hangzhou: hahng-jo
he: huh
Hongzhi Zhengjue: hung-jer jəng-jweh
hua: hwa
Huainanzi: hwhy-nan-ʤə

Huang: hwahng
Huangdi: hwang-dee
Huayan: hwa-yen
Huineng: hway-nɔng
jiao: jyow
junzi: jun-dʒɔ
Laozi: lao-dʒɔ
Li Er : lee ahr
liangzhi: lyahng-jer
Linghui: ling-hway
Liu: lyow (one syllable)
Liu Shu-hsien: lyo shu-shyen
Liu Xiang: lyoe shyahng
Lu Jiuyuan: loo jyo-yuan
Luoyang: law-yahng
Mao Zedong: mao dʒe-dong
Mazu Daoyi: mah-tsu dow-yi
Mazu: ma-tsu
Meizhou: may-jo
Meng Ke: mung kɔ
Mengzi: mung-dʒɔ
Mile: mee-lɔ
mixin: mee-shin
mofa: maw-fah
Mou Zongsan: mo dʒong-san
mozhao: maw-jow
nianfo: nyen-faw
Ningbo: ning-baw
Ouyang Xiu: oh-yahng shyo
po: paw
qi: chee
qian: chyen
Qin: chin
qing: ching
Qingming: ching-ming
Qiu: chyo
qizhi zhi xing: chee-jer jɔ shing
Quanzhen: chwan-jɔn
Qufu: choo-foo
Qunqiu: chun-chyo
Sanqing: san-ching
Shang: shahng
Shangdi: shahng-dee
Shangqing: shahng-ching
Shenhui: shun-hway
Shennong: shun-nung
Shenxiu: shun-shyo
Shijiamouni: sher-jyah-mo-ni

shijie: sher-jyeh
Shijing: sher-jing
Shitou Xiqian: sher-toe shee-chyen
si: sɔ
Sima Guang: sɔ-mah gwahng
Sui: sway
Taiqing: tai-ching
taixi: tai-shee
Taixu: tai-shü
Tang: tahng
Tian: tyen (one syllable)
Tiancun: tyen-tsun
tianli: tyen-lee
Tianshi: tyen-sher
Tiantai: tyen-tai
Tu Weiming: du way-ming
Tzu Chi: tsɔ-jee
wang: wahng
Wang Anshi: wahng ahn-sher
Wang Zhe: wahng jɔ
wei: way
Wen: wun
wushi: woo-sher
wuwei: woo-way
wuxing: woo-shing
Xia: shia
Xian: shee-an
xiangfa: shyahng-fah
xiao: shyao
xin: shin
xing: shing
Xiong Shili: shyung sher-lee
Xiongnu: shyong-nu
xu: shü
Xu Fuguan: shü foo-gwan
Xuan: shwan
Xuanzang: shwan-dʒahng
xue: shweh
Xunzi: shun-dʒɔ
Yan Hui: yen hway
yang: yahng
Yang Xi: yahng shee
Yangzi: yahng-dʒɔ
Yijing: yee-jing
Yixuan: yee-shwan
Zaojun: dʒow-jun
Zhang Junmai : jahng jun-mai
Zhang Zai: jahng tsai

Zhao: jow
Zhaozhou Congshen: jow-jo tsong-shen
zheng: jɔng
zhengfa: jɔng-fah
Zhengyi: jɔng-yi
zhenren: jɔn-ren
zhi liangzhi: jer lyahng-jer
Zhiyi: jer-yi
zhong: jung
Zhongni: jung-ni
Zhongyong: jung-yung

Zhou: jo
Zhu Xi: joo shee
Zhuangzi: jwahng-dʒə
zihua: dʒə-hwa
ziran: dʒə-ran
Zou Yan: dʒoe yen
zu: dʒoo
zuochan: dʒaw-chahn
zuowang: dʒaw-wahng
zuxian: dʒoo-shyen

Chinese Festivals

people went out in boats to find his body and threw *zongzi* (steamed rice wrapped in leaves) into the river to appease the river god, so that fish would not desecrate his body. Today there are hugely popular dragon-boat races (some are even held by Chinese communities in the United States), and *zongzi* are eaten.

6/24   **Birthday of Guandi**, god of war.

7/15   **Ghost Festival**. This entire month is known as Ghost Month, when the gates of hell are open and ghosts can mingle with the living. The festival on the 15th includes a communal feast to which wandering ghosts, as well as living beggars, are invited. This was originally a Buddhist festival, but is now part of popular religion.

8/15   **Mid-Autumn Festival**, celebrating the autumn harvest. "Moon-cakes" are commonly eaten.

8/27   **Birthday of Confucius**, celebrated in Taiwan every year on September 28.

9/9   **Double Yang Day**. Since in *Yijing* divination the number nine yields an unbroken, or *yang*, line—and all odd numbers are *yang*—this day is deemed to be auspicious.

10/5   **Birthday of Bodhidharma.**

11/17   **Birthday of Amitabha Buddha.**

12/8   **Celebration of the enlightenment of Sakyamuni Buddha.**

12/23   **Stove God reports to the Jade Emperor.**

Suggested Further Reading

Chapter 1

WM. THEODORE DE BARY and IRENE BLOOM (eds), *Sources of Chinese Tradition*, 2nd ed., 2 vols. (New York: Columbia University Press, 1999–2000) A comprehensive collection of texts covering Chinese history, philosophy, and religion from ancient times to the present.

DONALD S. LOPEZ, JR. (ed.), *Religions of China in Practice* (Princeton: Princeton University Press, 1996) Less-mainstream texts, focusing on religious practice.

SUSAN NAQUIN and CHÜN-FANG YÜ (eds), *Pilgrims and Sacred Sites in China* (Berkeley: University of California Press, 1992) Scholarly articles on pilgrimage in China, from Buddhist and Daoist sacred mountains to Mao's tomb.

Chapter 2

K.C. CHANG, *Art, Myth, and Ritual: The Path to Political Authority in Ancient China* (Cambridge: Harvard University Press, 1983) An accessible study of the Shang and Zhou periods by one of the leading archaeologists of ancient China.

DAVID N. KEIGHTLEY, *Sources of Shang History: The Oracle Bone Inscriptions of Bronze Age China* (Berkeley: University of California Press, 1978) The leading American historian of the Shang dynasty introduces both the general reader and the specialist to the art of deciphering Shang oracle bones.

——, *The Ancestral Landscape: Time, Space, and Community in Late Shang China, ca. 1200–1045 B.C.* (Berkeley: Institute of East Asian Studies, University of California, 2000) Aspects of Shang culture, deduced from the oracle bones and other archaeological finds.

MU-CHOU POO, *In Search of Personal Welfare: A View of Ancient Chinese Religion* (Albany: State University of New York Press, 1998) A ground-breaking study of popular religion during the Zhou dynasty.

Chapter 3

MARK CSIKSZENTMIHALYI and PHILIP J. IVANHOE (eds), *Religious and Philosophical Aspects of Laozi* (Albany: State University of New York Press, 1999) A collection of scholarly interpretations of the *Laozi*.

A.C. GRAHAM, *Disputers of the Tao: Philosophical Argument in Ancient China* (LaSalle, IL: Open Court, 1989) One of the best twentieth-century historians and interpreters of Chinese philosophy synthesizes its early history.

PHILIP J. IVANHOE and Bryan W. Van Norden (eds), *Readings in Classical Chinese Philosophy* (New York and London: Seven Bridges Press, 2001) Extensive selections from the major thinkers of the classical period.

BENJAMIN I. SCHWARTZ, *The World of Thought in Ancient China* (Cambridge, MA: Harvard University Press, 1985) An excellent history of classical Chinese political and religious thought, with a comparative perspective.

TU WEI-MING, *Humanity and Self-cultivation: Essays in Confucian Thought* (1980; rpt. Boston: Cheng & Tsui Co., 1998) A collection of essays by a pre-eminent contemporary Confucian scholar.

TU WEIMING and MARY EVELYN TUCKER (eds), *Confucian Spirituality I* (New York: Crossroad Publishing [forthcoming]) The first of a two-volume collection of essays focusing on the "inner" dimensions of Confucian religious practice; part of a series on "World Spirituality."

XINZHONG YAO, *An Introduction to Confucianism* (Cambridge: Cambridge University Press, 2000) An excellent historical and topical introduction to Confucianism as a religious and philosophical tradition.

Chapter 4

STEPHEN R. BOKENKAMP, *Early Daoist Scriptures* (Berkeley: University of California Press, 1997) A selection of translations from the three major scriptural traditions of the Daoist religion, with very helpful introductions.

CHENG CHIEN BHIKSHU, *Sun Face Buddha: The Teachings of Ma-tsu and the Hung-chou School of Ch'an* (Berkeley: Asian Humanities Press, 1992) The recorded sayings of the forerunner of the Linji school of Chan Buddhism, with an excellent introduction.

HEINRICH DUMOULIN, *Zen Buddhism: A History*, vol. 1: *India and China* (New York and London: Macmillan, 1988) The first of a standard two-volume history of Chan/Zen Buddhism (the second volume covers Japan).

LIVIA KOHN (ed.), *Taoist Meditation and Longevity Techniques* (Ann Arbor: Center for Chinese Studies, 1989) A collection of scholarly essays on various Daoist traditions of meditation and self-cultivation.

—, *Daoism and Chinese Culture* (Cambridge, MA: Three Pines Press, 2001) An excellent introduction to the Daoist religion.

WILLIAM F. POWELL (trans.), *The Record of Tung-shan* (Honolulu: University of Hawaii Press, 1986) The recorded sayings of one of the founders of the Caodong school of Chan Buddhism, with an excellent introduction.

Chapter 5

PATRICIA BUCKLEY EBREY and PETER N. GREGORY (eds), *Religion and Society in T'ang and Sung China* (Honolulu: University of Hawaii Press, 1993) A collection of scholarly essays on various aspects of Chinese religious practice.

JACQUES GERNET, *China and the Christian Impact*, trans. Janet Lloyd (Cambridge: Cambridge University Press, 1985) A study of the conflict between Christian missionary teachings and the traditional Chinese worldview.

PETER N. GREGORY and DANIEL A. GETZ, JR., *Buddhism in the Sung* (Honolulu: University of Hawaii Press, 1999) Another collection of essays, arguing against the traditional idea that Chinese Buddhism reached its peak in the Tang dynasty.

VALERIE HANSEN, *Changing Gods in Medieval China, 1127–1276* (Princeton: Princeton University Press, 1990) An excellent study of Chinese popular religion during the Song dynasty.

TAIGEN DANIEL LEIGHTON with YI WU (trans.), *Cultivating the Empty Field: The Silent Illumination of Zen Master Hongzhi* (San Francisco: North Point Press, 1991) The recorded sayings of the leading Song-dynasty exponent of the Caodong school of Chan Buddhism, with an excellent introduction.

KIDDER SMITH, JR., PETER K. BOL, JOSEPH A. ADLER, and DON J. WYATT, *Sung Dynasty Uses of the "I Ching"* (Princeton: Princeton University Press, 1990) A study of the major Song Neo-Confucian interpretations of the *Classic of Change*.

RICHARD J. SMITH, *Fortune-Tellers and Philosophers: Divination in Traditional Chinese Society* (Boulder, CO: Westview Press, 1991) An excellent study of the various forms of Chinese divination, focusing on the Qing dynasty.

TU WEIMING and MARY EVELYN TUCKER (eds), *Confucian Spirituality II* (New York: Crossroad Publishing [forthcoming]) The second volume on Confucianism in the "World Spirituality" series, covering the Neo-Confucian and modern periods.

Chapter 6

DAVID K. JORDAN, *Gods, Ghosts, and Ancestors: Folk Religion in a Taiwanese Village* (Berkeley: University of California Press, 1972) An anthropological study of popular religion in Taiwan, based on fieldwork done in the 1960s.

MICHAEL SASO, *Taoism and the Rite of Cosmic Renewal*, 2nd ed. (Pullman: Washington State University Press, 1990) A study of the *jiao* ritual in contemporary Taiwan.

MEIR SHAHAR and ROBERT P. WELLER (eds), *Unruly Gods: Divinity and Society in China* (Honolulu: University of Hawaii Press, 1996) A collection of essays on popular religion from the Song to modern times.

ROBERT P. WELLER, *Unities and Diversities in Chinese Religion* (Seattle: University of Washington Press, 1987) An anthropological study of popular religion in Taiwan, focusing on the Ghost Festival.

ARTHUR P. WOLF (ed.), *Religion and Ritual in Chinese Society* (Stanford: Stanford University Press, 1974) A seminal collection of scholarly essays on popular religion.

Internet Resources

Websites can be somewhat ephemeral; the following list of useful Internet addresses was accurate at the time of going to press:

http://sun.sino.uni-heidelberg.de/igcs/igphil.htm
The Internet Guide for Chinese Studies (Heidelberg University), Philosophy and Religion page.

http://religion.rutgers.edu/SSCR/linksrel.html
Links page maintained by the Society for the Study of Chinese Religions.

http://www-chaos.umd.edu/history/toc.html
A short history of China.

http://helios.unive.it/~dsao//pregadio/index.html
"The Golden Elixir," website on Chinese alchemy.

http://pears2.lib.ohio-state.edu/e-CBS.htm
"Digital Buddhist Library and Museum," Center for Buddhist Studies at National Taiwan University, with material in English, Chinese, Pali, Sanskrit, and Tibetan.

An extensive and regularly updated list of Internet links can be found on the following website, maintained by the author:
http://www2.kenyon.edu/depts/religion/fac/adler/reln270/links270.htm

Index